TURKEY

TIME-LIFE BOOKS/AMSTERDAM

COOKERY AROUND THE WORLD
TURKEY

FUNDA ENGIN

Food photography: Michael Brauner

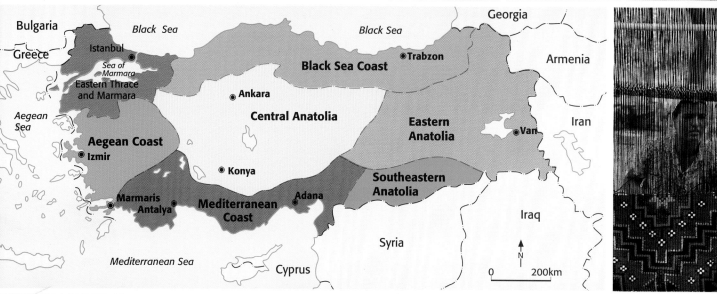

Bulgaria	Black Sea	Georgia
Greece		
Istanbul	Black Sea Coast	Armenia
Sea of Marmara	Trabzon	
Eastern Thrace and Marmara	Ankara	Iran
Aegean Sea	Central Anatolia	Eastern Anatolia
Aegean Coast		Van
Izmir	Konya	
		Southeastern Anatolia
Marmaris	Adana	Iraq
Antalya	Mediterranean Coast	Syria
Mediterranean Sea	Cyprus	N
		0 200km

CONTENTS

TURKEY: THE LAND OF MANY DELIGHTS

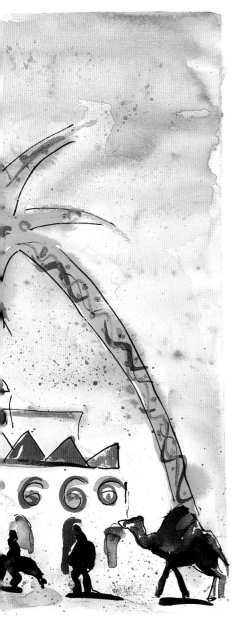

To stroll through the streets of Istanbul without stopping for a meal here or a bite of a delicious snack there is virtually impossible. From the little bars dotted around the great Blue Mosque comes the tempting smell of grilled meatballs; while from the boats bobbing on the Golden Horn wafts the aroma of sea-fresh fried fish. On the neighbouring quayside, street traders sell tasty fried sardines, sandwiched between crusty bread, and small stalls offer spicy *lahmacun*, a type of Turkish pizza. Yet further temptation for the tastebuds is offered by the nearby Egyptian Market, where piles of vegetables, fruit, fish, cheese and olives are temptingly displayed, and sacks of spices, dried culinary herbs, and different kinds of tea create a dazzling blaze of colour.

Wandering around Istanbul provides an ideal introduction to the cookery and culinary culture of this hospitable land. If you order a selection of appetizers—known as *meze*—in one of the many speciality restaurants, or sample one of the typical regional dishes, it is not hard to see why Turkish cuisine ranks among the best in the world.

Throughout history, many cultures and races have contributed towards making Turkish cookery what it is today. It began around 8,000 years ago, when one of civilization's earliest urban settlements was established at Çatal Höyük in central Anatolia. Over the course of several thousand years, the country was overrun by succeeding waves of foreign invaders, who brought with them their own culinary traditions, thereby enriching the native cuisine with exotic spices and unfamiliar ingredients. Alongside the simple daily fare of the farmers and shepherds, Istanbul saw the development of the sophisticated culinary art of the sultan's palace, which benefited, too, from the wealth and variety of Turkey's own agricultural products.

To a large degree, the inhabitants of present-day Turkey still live off the land. As well as cotton and tobacco, the export of fruit and vegetables also provides a valuable source of revenue. Indeed, throughout the world, wherever Turkish traders have settled, their shops have acquired a reputation for wonderfully fresh vegetables.

The Turkish people are famed for their friendliness and warm-hearted hospitality—a characteristic that is symbolized by the small, tulip-shaped glasses of black tea with which guests or prospective customers are always welcomed—at any time of day. In rural areas, instead of hot tea, visitors are offered *ayran* (a chilled yogurt drink) or a piece of fruit as refreshment.

This book will appeal especially to readers who have returned from Turkey with lasting impressions of this legendary hospitality, and of the delicious food and drink. The first chapter provides a brief introduction to the country and its people, and to their traditions, festivals and favourite foods. This is followed by seven chapters of authentic Turkish recipes, arranged in the order of a traditional Turkish menu. Cooking is made easy with practical step-by-step instructions, which are complemented by illustrations of the more complicated techniques. In addition, there are helpful notes and variations on the recipes themselves, and information on some of the more important ingredients. Finally, there is a list of suggested menu combinations and a glossary of some Turkish culinary words and expressions, all of which will enable you to entertain your guests in true—and informed—Turkish style.

So, bring the flavours of the orient into your own home, and enjoy the many delicious and exotic specialities of this enchanting country!

WHERE EAST MEETS WEST

Turkey covers an area of approximately 780,000 square kilometres. The larger part of the country—97 per cent—occupies a huge peninsula enclosed by the Black Sea, the Sea of Marmara, the Aegean and the Mediterranean. Known today as Anatolia, it belongs, geographically speaking, to Asia. The remaining three per cent, lying in the northwestern corner of the country, is part of Europe, making Istanbul, with a population of 12 million inhabitants, the only city in the world to straddle two continents.

Given its size and location, Turkey necessarily embraces a number of contrasting climatic zones, which have over the centuries affected local life, agriculture and cookery. Along the Mediterranean and Aegean coasts, where hot summers alternate with mild winters, subtropical temperatures and lush vegetation predominate. Central, southeastern and eastern Anatolia have a continental climate, with prolonged periods of heat and cold. The land here is parched in summer and, in eastern Anatolia, is covered in snow until the spring. Along the shores of the Black Sea it often rains, and the mountains never lose their lush green covering.

This wide range of landscape and climate is reflected in the variety of Turkey's agricultural produce, which in turn accounts for the diversity of Turkish cuisine. The country's culinary tradition is a long one. The origins of Anatolian cuisine were uncovered among the ruins of Çatal Höyük—an urban settlement founded more than 8,000 years ago—when evidence was revealed of highly developed domestic animal husbandry and agriculture. Turkey's subsequent history bears the marks of the many different races and cultures that have inhabited its lands, some of whom have strongly influenced the nation's cookery. Many vegetable and fish dishes date back to Byzantine times, while dishes such as vegetables stuffed with rice, raisins and nuts are a legacy of the Armenians of eastern Turkey. Yogurt and kebabs were among the contributions of the Turkish tribes from the Steppes of central Asia, the forebears of present-day Turks.

The versatility of Turkish cuisine is due not only to these many centuries of influences, but also to the differences between rural and urban styles of cooking—for example, many women in rural areas still bake their bread daily on dome-shaped baking sheets over a small fire. At the same time, there is a wide range of seasonal and regional dishes, which provide yet further year-round variety—all of which makes getting to know the people of Turkey and their food an exciting, and constantly surprising, experience.

The six slender minarets of the magnificent Blue Mosque are one of the most magical sights on Istanbul's horizon. The mosque's name derives from the decorative tiles that adorn its interior.

Eastern Thrace and Marmara

Sunflowers, wine and cakes—fare fit for a sultan

The little triangle of land that constitutes European Turkey, once part of the ancient country of Thrace, is bounded by frontiers with Greece and Bulgaria and extends as far as Istanbul. Characterized by vineyards, fields of sunflowers, and pastureland, it is a region of gentle hills, undulating in long waves down to the Dardanelles and the Sea of Marmara, which forms a natural border between Europe and Asia.

As the gateway to the orient, this tiny part of Turkey has always been strategically important: in 334 BC, Alexander the Great crossed the Dardanelles and first set foot on Asian soil, and in the late 13th century, the Ottomans, whose great empire in Europe, Asia and Africa was to last until the end of the first world war, invaded the region from the Balkans.

Edirne, now the provincial capital, became the glittering headquarters of the Ottoman sultans, who erected the magnificent Selimiye Mosque (1528-66) and the bazaar complex. In the narrow streets of Edirne, traditional crafts still flourish: broom-makers; belt-makers—whose wares include fabulous bridles—and smiths can be seen in their little workshops. The town is also famous for its wrestling festival (June/July). The participants, who are smothered with oil before the contest, come from all over Turkey to compete.

European Turkey is one of the country's most important wine-growing areas, and the industry is centred on Tekirdag, on the Sea of Marmara. The region's temperate climate produces mainly dry, but also medium-dry, wines; the reds are full of character and the whites fresh and fruity. Some of the grapes grown here are used for making *rakı*, a fiery, aniseed-flavoured spirit frequently drunk with the evening meal.

Istanbul's palace cuisine

One of the undoubted culinary highlights of a tour through Turkey is the cuisine of Istanbul. Throughout the Ottoman Empire—a period of 450 years—the city attracted the highest calibre cooks from east and west, who derived their inspiration from the highly refined cuisine practised at the palace of the sultans. The magnificent Topkapi Palace, founded in 1459 by Sultan Mehmet II (conqueror of Constantinople), stands on a peninsula overlooking the Sea of Marmara. Here, exquisite meals were prepared daily for the sultan, his mother and his harem. The food was served on fabulous Chinese porcelain, which today forms one of the largest and most valuable collections of its kind in the world.

Each of the palace cooks had his own special area of expertise—pies, meat dishes or sweetmeats, for example—a trend that still characterizes Turkish catering. *Baklavaci* specialize in the delicious pastries knownas *baklava*, *işkembeci* specialize in tripe soup, while *börekçi* deal in flaky pasties with various fillings, and *muhallebici* concentrate on dairy foods such as the delicious scorched milk pudding.

These traditional shops and restaurants are a familiar sight in the Aksaray, the old quarter of the city, and can also be found in the districts between the Golden Horn inlet and the Bosphorus. Istanbul is also famous for its markets, which provide the city with vegetables, fruit, fish, meat, cheese, olives, nuts and spices, as well as many regional specialities: be sure to visit the Egyptian Market, located by the Galata Bridge, and the Flower Market, (on İstiklal Caddesi in the Pera

district), which is overlooked by the tomb of Ahmet III, known as the Tulip King. Among restaurants offering food in the great Ottoman tradition are "Pandeli", situated in the Egyptian Market building, and "Darüzziyafe", near the lovely Süleymaniye Mosque.

Fertile Marmara

Across the Sea of Marmara, in Anatolia (formerly Asia Minor), fruit, vegetables and wine are added to this region's rich array of produce. The countryside around the city of Bursa, for example, is particularly famous for its potatoes, onions and luscious peaches, and sweet chestnuts and jams are popular souvenirs of a visit here.

The Ottomans made Bursa their first capital in 1326 (before Edirne and Istanbul, which fell in 1361 and 1453 respectively); among the legacies of the city's golden age are the Grand Mosque, the Green Mosque, and the sultan's family mausoleum. Today, this busy commercial city is renowned as a health resort because of its thermal

Shoppers engage in a lively discussion in the busy arcades of the Egyptian Market, near Istanbul's Galata Bridge.

A stallholder cheerfully tosses a handful of silkworm cocoons into the air. Kozan Han, Bursa's silk market, supplies the raw material for the region's exquisite silk carpets.

Shaded from the searing midday heat beneath a tree, workers thread tobacco leaves onto thin sticks and lay them out to dry.

Rugged stone walls and sun-bleached pavements serve as the perfect display case for these beautiful hand-knotted Bergama carpets.

springs, and for its winter sports resorts, based around the nearby Ulu Dag mountain. It is also a traditional centre of the silk industry, and the locally bred silkworms provide the raw material for the exquisite carpets manufactured in the workshops of Hereke and Istanbul. Another fascinating little walled town, north of Bursa, is Iznik, the ancient Nicaea. It was here, in potteries set up under the Ottomans, that the tiles decorating many of the country's finest mosques and other buildings were produced.

Aegean Coast and Hinterland

Olives and ancient treasures

The scenery along the Aegean coast is one of alternating mountains and plains. Over the course of thousands of years, rivers such as the Greater and Lesser Maeander flooded the fertile soil of their estuaries, gradually silting up Ephesus and Miletus, the ancient world's most famous harbours, which had subsequently to be abandoned. This flooded land was a godsend to succeeding generations, however, for it permitted the cultivation of cotton, tobacco, wine and vegetables, all of

which have contributed to the prosperity of the region. Olive trees, their silvery leaves glittering in the sun, cover the hills and mountainsides, providing a striking contrast to the rust and ochre hues of the soil. Two-thirds of the olive oil consumed in Turkey is produced on the north Aegean coast—vegetable dishes prepared with olive oil are particularly popular here—as is a large proportion of the country's pickled fruit. It is this region that supplies breakfast tables throughout Turkey with lush black olives.

There are many ancient ruins here, serving as a reminder of the coast's turbulent past. Among them is the legendary city of Troy—situated where the Dardanelles flow into the Aegean—whose story is told in Homer's epic, the *Iliad*. Equally famous is Pergamum (Bergama), which in Grecian times possessed the greatest library of the ancient world. Archaeologists still find plenty to occupy them at the imposing mountain fortress which dominates the little town today. Monday is market day, when the streets are enlivened by the local farmers' brightly painted horse-drawn carts. Between late May and early June an international festival of music, folklore, exhibitions and theatre takes place here. And Bergama's renowned hand-made carpets are a year-round attraction.

Ancient and modern İzmir

The Turks affectionately call their third-largest city *Güzel İzmir*, beautiful İzmir. With almost three million inhabitants, and a constant stream of immigrants from southeastern and eastern Anatolia—not to mention the influx of tourists—the ancient city of

Smyrna is today bursting at the seams, causing its environment to suffer as a consequence. Admittedly, there is little evidence of this along the Atatürk Caddesi, with its tall palm trees, marble villas, imposing office and bank buildings, designer boutiques, bars and deluxe restaurants. Horse-drawn cabs, quietly waiting for customers, bring a touch of nostalgia and Levantine calm.

The same is true of the narrow streets of the old town, at the foot of the ancient citadel, Kadifekale. Here, the sound of hammer blows rings out from shoemaker's workshops, men in the teahouses draw lazily on their water pipes, and playing pieces clatter on the *tavla*—backgammon boards. In the nearby Kemeraltı market, where gold rings and bracelets glitter from jewellers' shop windows, fish merchants extol the virtues of the night's catch, herb-sellers promote their miraculous medicines and women tempt the passing tourists with their beautifully printed fabrics. Be sure to buy some figs here, too; Turkey is famous for its figs, the best of which are grown around Izmir. Inland, the nearby town of Manisa, home to some notable mosques, is the site of the annual Mesir Festival (dates vary from year to year), with its agricultural fair and folklore displays.

A picturesque island world; a fairy-tale fortress

The coast of the northern and southern Aegean is renowned for its many holiday resorts, including Çandarlı, Foça, Çeşme, Kuşadası and Bodrum, all of

The limestone rockpools of Pamukkale make a stunning sight as they glitter in the sunlight.

Yacht masts and minarets mingle on the horizon in Bodrum's pretty harbour.

A catamaran, its sail billowing in the wind, glides majestically past an idyllic beach near Fethiye, on the Ölü Deniz lagoon.

them blessed with lovely bathing beaches as well as many fascinating historical sights, including a number of very fine castles.

Beneath the crusader castle of St Peter, in Bodrum harbour, the masts of the yachts sway against a backdrop of square, white, Mediterranean-style houses. This is the point of departure for the "Blue Voyage", a sailing trip around the coves and islands between Bodrum and Marmaris. The boat anchors for meals wherever the skipper chooses, whereupon he displays his excellent culinary skills.

Situated inland close to Denizli—and easily reached by bus—is one of Turkey's most extraordinary natural phenomena, Pamukkale, or "Cotton Castle". Here, on a mountainside, the deposits of mineral-rich hot-water springs have created a white, fairy-tale fortress of calcareous rocks and circular pools, the whole seemingly made of fluffy cotton—hence the name.

The ruins of Hierapolis are a reminder that the Romans once came to take the waters here. Nowadays, the baths are the site of a museum, and it is the feet of the many visiting tourists, rather than gladiators, which now raise the dust in the amphitheatre's arena.

The Mediterranean Coast

The Toros Mountains and blue bays

To the west of the popular tourist resort of Marmaris, set picturesquely in a bay beneath the ruins of Ottoman fortifications, the narrow Reşadiye peninsula extends like a long, thin finger into the sea. At its tip lies the ancient town of Cnidus; founded by the Greeks, it was the centre of a cult to the goddess Aphrodite. In the centre of the peninsula—which is only about 800 metres wide—is the village of Datça, a paradise for divers and sailors. Among the many other attractions of the region are the remains of the Carian city of Caunus, and the nearby Dalyan nature reserve, whose labyrinth of waterways winds between reed-covered islands which are home to rare flora and fauna. Here, set in cliffs high above the water, a number of ancient rock- and temple-tombs can be seen.

A large part of the Mediterranean coast is dominated by the Toros mountain range. The long coastal road twists and turns its way perilously along the mountainsides—some of them falling sheer into the sea— revealing one breathtakingly beautiful view after another. The green of the pinewoods that clothe the slopes offsets the spectacular blue of the bays and lagoons, one of the loveliest of which is at Ölü Deniz, near Fethiye.

On the fertile, well-watered plain that surrounds this little town, vegetables, tobacco, grapes and cotton are grown; and in the steep clearings among the pines stand blue hives full of the honey bees that produce the delicious local thyme and wild-flower honey.

Traces of the past around Antalya

Many ancient ruins can be found along the coast, reminders of the tribes who once settled here—Carians, Lycians, and Pisidians all built cities along Grecian lines. Centuries later, glorious Byzantine churches were added to this rich architectural mosaic, as well as the magnificent edifices of the Ottoman Empire. Among the sites worth visiting are the great Lycian city of Xanthus, Kaş (Antiphellus) and Myra.

The main tourist attraction—and the largest town on Turkey's south coast— is Antalya, which rises proudly above the sea on a rocky plateau. Entry to the town is through a Roman gate, built in honour of the Emperor Hadrian, and the restored old centre is distinguished by the fluted minaret dating from the time of the Seljuk Turks. Another treasure is the harbour beneath the old city walls; here you can find gourmet restaurants offering such local fish specialities as sea bass parcels and swordfish kebabs, all wonderfully fresh. Restaurants around the market offer plain and simple local dishes such as bean salad with sesame dressing, or grilled kebabs. The local jams—made from figs, aubergines, rose petals and quinces—are popular as souvenirs.

Turkish riviera

The area between Antalya and Alanya is popularly known as the Turkish Riviera. Its sandy beaches, extending for several kilometres, are much in demand, as are its bays, hotels and holiday villages in resorts such as Kemer, where the landscape is filled with orange and lemon groves, and Side, whose 2nd-century theatre is one of the most interesting in Turkey. Scattered along the coast beyond Alanya are a number of stately castles, the most imposing of which is found four kilometres inland at Anamur. Another of the region's draws is its subtropical climate, which attracts visitors year-round. On little terraces overlooking the sea behind Alanya, bananas are cultivated, and in autumn the date palms are decked with the bright red bunches of ripening fruit.

Excursions into the mountainous hinterland lead to unspoilt villages and to the *yayla*, the cool, high plateaus where shepherds and their families pitch their brown, goatskin tents to

These Lycian cliff tombs, carved into the rock face high above the water, can be admired on a boat trip through the Dalyan nature reserve.

A market seller holds aloft a great bunch of red chili peppers—the source of Turkish food's characteristic spicy flavour.

Bizarre "fairy chimneys", shaped over many centuries by the wind and rain, lend an otherworldly feel to the landscape of the valley of Göreme in Cappadocia.

escape the heat of summer. Extending beyond Mersin, Turkey's largest Mediterranean port, is the vast plain of Çukurova, with the agricultural and industrial centre of Adana. Here, where the temperatures in summer soar to over 40°C, cotton and citrus fruits thrive, as do the small hot chilis that make the local kebabs so fiery.

Central Anatolia

Fairy chimneys and a whiff of garlic

For those who like peering into cooking pots, ancient or modern, Turkey is the ideal destination, and in this respect its museums are very exciting. Among their many fascinating exhibits are clay vessels more than 8,000 years old containing tiny scraps of cereals—emmer, einkorn, barley and wheat—that give an insight into the diet of the country's earliest inhabitants. In 1958, in central Anatolia, the British archaeologist James Mellaart uncovered the remains of Çatal Höyük, one of the world's oldest urban settlements. Among his finds were 14 different cultivated plants, including peas and beans, as well as a collection of kitchen utensils.

Throughout the ages, central Anatolia has been the meeting point for many races: Assyrians, Hittites, Phrygians, Greeks, Romans and the Seljuks, the first Turkish tribe to settle here in the 11th century. Many Turkish clans originated from central Asia, from where small clans or large ethnic groups, including the Huns, had moved westwards over the centuries in search of new grazing lands, or eager for fresh conquests. The present-day Turks are descended from these tribes and from peoples already settled in Asia Minor.

Modern trunk roads still follow the old trade routes, which, like the Silk Road, linked Europe and Asia. One leads from the coast close to Antalya through the mountains into the highlands, passing lakes and ancient caravanserais (caravan inns). At the edge of the high, sun-drenched plateaus of central Anatolia, Turkey's corn bowl, stands the bustling town of Konya, site of the country's most important Islamic shrine.

When the Seljuks arrived in 1071, they found an already thriving city (Iconium, inhabited by Byzantine Christians), which they proceeded to establish as the capital of their Sultanate of Rum. It was the Seljuks who brought Islam to Asia Minor. Sultan Alâeddin Keykubad I (1219-1236) was a brilliant ruler, who equipped his empire and its capital with splendid mosques, *medrese* (institutes of higher education) and caravanserais: these Seljuk buildings, with their chiselled portals and their minarets richly decorated with faïence, are much admired today.

At Konya, during the Sultan's reign, the mystic, Mevlâna Celâleddin-i Rûmî, founded the order of the Whirling Dervishes. The kitchens of the order's monastery (now a museum) were once the domain of one Ateş Baz-i-Veli, the Guardian Master Cook. Today, women still make the pilgrimage to his tomb, taking home with them a pinch of the salt distributed there to bless their own culinary efforts. The annual Whirling Dervish Festival, celebrated from 14 to 17 December, attracts visitors from all over the world.

Ankara and Cappadocia

In 1923, the Turkish general Kemal Atatürk, the father of modern Turkey, made Ankara the capital of his newly established Turkish republic. Since then, this sleepy, provincial town in central Anatolia has grown into a thoroughly modern city housing several million inhabitants, with many ancient buildings and long, elegant boulevards. Ankara's Archaelogical Museum houses fascinating relics of the Hittite era (the Hittites were a migrant Indo-germanic people who dominated most of Anatolia between 1900 and 1200 BC), including an outstanding collection of clay tablets engraved with cuneiform script. These were unearthed—and deciphered—by the German Assyriologist Hugo Winckler who, at the beginning of the 20th century, excavated the site of the Hittite capital Hattuşaş, some 200 kilometres east of Ankara. From his work it was learnt that the Hittites brewed beer from grain.

One of Turkey's most amazing natural wonders lies in the heart of central Anatolia in Cappadocia. Many millions of years ago, a group of volcanoes, the highest of which are Hasan Dağı (3,253 metres) and Erciyas Dağı (3,916 metres), erupted, scattering great quantities of ash, rock and lava over a wide area. Erosion, and the effects of sun, wind and rain, then created in the

A splash of green, and the snow-capped slopes of the extinct volcano Erciyas Dağı, add a touch of life to an otherwise bleak landscape.

Picking chick-peas is a back-breaking task for these Anatolian peasant women.

hidden valleys a fabulous, fairy-tale land of pyramids of earth and cones of volcanic rock—which the locals call fairy chimneys—into which dwellings have been carved. Cappadocia is a very secluded area, with extraordinarily fertile soil. As a result, it has long attracted groups of settlers, in particular such persecuted groups as Christians, and also hermits, for whom it became a safe haven. In the soft volcanic stone they dug cave dwellings, churches, which they decorated with frescoes, and monasteries. Around the borders of the area, underground cities on several levels were created.

The appeal of Cappadocia lies not only in the strange beauty of its landscape and villages, but also in the friendliness of the inhabitants in popular tourist centres such as Ürgüp and Göreme. Visitors should certainly sample the Cappadocian wines, which frequently win prizes at the Ürgüp Wine Festival in October. And many of the shops here sell the hand-knotted carpets and woven *kilims* typical of central Anatolia. In nearby Avanos— which hosts a craft festival in August

A dazzling orange mosaic of Cappadocian apricots lies drying in the sun. As the water evaporates, the plump fruit gradually shrink, and darken in colour.

and is renowned for its pottery—wine pitchers and cooking pots for *güveç*, a meat and vegetable stew, are sold.

At the foot of the extinct volcano Erciyas stands the town of Kayseri and its citadel, where the Romans and the Seljuks left a legacy of some fine buildings as reminders of their golden age, among them some outstanding mausoleums. Now a centre of the carpet industry, Kayseri also produces *pastırma*, air-dried loin of beef seasoned with garlic. Watch out when you are buying it though—the townspeople are skilled hagglers!

Southeastern and Eastern Anatolia

A mountain of the gods, and the sacred carp

The region of Anatolia that borders with Syria and Iraq enjoys some of the hottest temperatures in the country: the towns of Diyarbakır and Şanlıurfa, which lie close to the plain of Harran, bask at more than 40° in the shade in early summer. By contrast, the statues of the gods on the 2,100-metre-high peak of Mount Nemrut keep a cool head all the year round. From this vantage point you can gaze into the far distance over a series of beautiful mountain peaks. King Antiochus I of Commagene (*c*.69—*c*.32 BC) actually chose to be buried on the summit, in order to be closer to heaven.

The waters of the rivers Tigris and Euphrates collect in the mountain valleys, forming large reservoirs which provide the water to irrigate the sun-drenched but fertile plain of Harran. The town of Gaziantep, near the Syrian

frontier, is renowned for its pistachio nuts, which are gathered from the bushy trees that cover the surrounding countryside. As well as being delicious eaten raw, pistachio nuts are used in fillings for cakes and chicken rolls, and confectioners turn them into distinctive green marzipan. Gaziantep is a modern commercial centre with a thriving tradition in handicrafts: brass- and copperware, fabric for traditional costumes and inlaid mother-of-pearl artefacts are all manufactured in the old quarters of the town.

The towns of Haran and Şanlıurfa, on the northern edge of the lowland plain of Mesopotamia, carry strong biblical associations: it was at the latter that Abraham and his wife Sarah are said to have camped beside a spring on their way from Ur to Canaan. The faithful make pilgrimages to the site, which lies below the spur on which the city sits, pausing to feed chick-peas and lettuce to the large shoal of sacred carp that

swim in several connecting pools, descendants of fish that were living in Abraham's time.

Southeastern Anatolia is also famous for its thoroughbred horses, on show at the Şanlıurfa Equestrian Festival, held at the end of October. The town of Diyarbakır, which is almost completely encircled by its old Roman city walls, swarms with street traders, shoeshine boys, and women in colourful Kurdish traditional dress. The town bazaar sells beautiful silver jewellery, and in summer the fruit stalls display Turkey's finest watermelons.

A harem, and Noah's landing place
Winters in eastern Anatolia are long and bitterly cold, and many of the mountain passes remain blocked until late spring. Life in this harsh mountain landscape is particularly arduous at this time of year, which is why its inhabitants greet spring and autumn with such enthusiasm. Once the snow

From their prominent hilltop setting, the ruins of the once magnificent 18th-century palace and mosque of İshak Paşa look out over the rocky valley close to Turkey's border with Iran.

Well protected against the heat of the day, workers sort through harvested tea leaves at Rize, at the eastern end of the Black Sea coast, the heart of Turkey's tea producing area.

has melted, the ground is carpeted with tulips, anemones and narcissuses. In autumn, the reds and rusts of the foliage add a vivid dash of colour to the groves of trees along the streams.

The undisputed natural wonder of the region is, of course, Mount Ararat, which continues to attract generations of travellers in search of adventure, as well as archaeologists seeking the place where Noah's Ark is said to have alighted after the Flood.

In the middle of eastern Anatolia lies Lake Van, Turkey's largest lake. Its banks are relatively bare, apart from a sprinkling of poplars, and walnut and apricot trees, and the great pyramids of "nomad's briquettes" (slices of dried cattle dung used as fuel) that are such a feature of the lakeside villages.

This region was ruled in turn by the Armenians, Georgians and Seljuks, who have all left a mark on the landscape. At Ahlat, there are some notable round *türbeler* (mausoleums) and carved gravestones. On a little island off the southwest bank of the lake stands the 10th-century Ahtamar church, a jewel of Armenian stone-carving. And the town of Van and habitations in the nearby high valleys still benefit from the irrigation system installed by the

Urartians, who controlled the area between the 9th and 6th centuries BC. In the bazaar in Van you will find on sale beautiful eastern Anatolian carpets and *kilims*, which sometimes provide a cosy resting place for the rare Van cats, a breed easily distinguished by their one blue and one green eye.

Cattle-rearing and the cultivation of sugar beet brought prosperity to the more northerly city of Erzurum, whose impressive buildings date from the Seljuk era. By contrast, the palace and harem of Ishak Paşa, which lies on a mountain plateau close to Turkey's border with Iran, radiates baroque exuberance. During the 17th century, the regional governor collected hefty road tolls from passing caravans and used them to finance the building of his fairy-tale castle.

The Black Sea Coast

Fish, tea and bullfights

Along the 1,200-kilometre coastline of the Black Sea lie many small, idyllic beaches where tourism is only now taking its first timid steps. Certainly, summer makes a briefer appearance here than in the west or south, and occasionally there are sudden showers. But the rain is beneficial, for it keeps the hillsides clothed in a brilliant green hue, which provides a perfect backdrop for the picturesque half-timbered houses typical of the region. These charming buildings, distinguished by their tall windows and doorways, have bays and ledges decorated in filigree woodwork. In amongst them, standing airily on stilts, are grain stores, with bright yellow corncobs peeking through the slats. In this part of the world, corn is used not only for feeding the ducks and geese, but also for making a very delicious cornmeal bread.

The towns and villages along the coast have very little room to expand, as the foothills of the Pontic and Kaçkar mountain ranges sweep almost down to the sea. Set on a peninsula in the west, Amasra, with its historic old town, was a Greek trading post in the 5th and 6th centuries BC, as were Sinop, Samsun, Giresun and Trabzon in the east. All of these towns possess buildings from different periods of their history, and appealing town centres with narrow streets. Perhaps the loveliest city along this stretch of coast is Trabzon, which still has a number of Byzantine churches and monasteries. It is also the starting point for excursions inland, including a visit to the Sumela Monastery, famous for its dramatic location and its frescos. During July and August, there are a number of alpine festivals to visit; particularly lively celebrations—including bullfighting—take place at the Çamli-hemşin-Ayder Festival (29-30 August). Silver jewellery, copperware, basketwork, wooden goods and fabrics are typical souvenirs to look out for.

Among the coast's principal sources of income are hazelnuts, and Turkey has become Europe's main supplier of these tasty nuts. The main growing area, the "Hazelnut Riviera", lies along the coast around Ordu. Between 19 and 22 September there is a hazelnut festival, complete with displays of local folklore. At the extreme eastern end of the Black sea coast are vast terraced tea plantations, which supply the Turks with their favourite drink, black tea.

The leaves are harvested from May onwards by women carrying huge panniers—quite a sight to see.

The Black Sea has a distinctive regional cuisine. One local speciality is *hamsi*, a silvery fish the size of a sardine; in season between November and February, it is served in a variety of ways. Another delicacy is turbot, usually sliced and deep-fried.

Home of the best cooks

Inland, to the west, the towns of Bolu and Mengen have, since Ottoman times, enjoyed an almost legendary reputation as the home of the finest cooks, and cookery contests are annually held here. Near Bolu lies Yedigöller Milli park, which boasts seven picturesque lakes set amongst forests of oak, elm and beech. It is one of 19 national parks in Turkey; designed to protect threatened plant and animal species, they also make perfect picnic spots.

Situated a few kilometres away from the coast are two of the best preserved towns built in the old Turkish style—

Spinning fibre by hand still forms a significant part of the daily routine for many women in rural areas.

A Black Sea fisherman patiently repairs a damaged section of net before beginning the day's work.

Kıymalı pide—yeast pastries filled with minced meat—are the delicacy on offer from this young street vendor, his wares balanced effortlessly on his head.

Safranbolu and Kastamonu—both of which are designated national monuments. Most of the splendid half-timbered villas, with their tiled, hipped roofs, date back to the 18th and 19th centuries; visitors are often astounded by just how comfortable and well designed these houses are, cool in summer and protected from the effects of wind and cold in winter.

The head of the household receives guests in the *selamlık*, which is the most beautiful room in the house. Family life, however, centres on the harem, where the wife is in charge. The floors are laid with beautiful carpets and *kilims*, and it is customary to remove one's shoes before entering.

In Safranbolu's little streets, you can see beadmakers at work, making the blue glass beads that are placed in homes and cars to ward off the evil eye. These beads are often sewn into children's clothes, to keep the wearers from coming to any harm.

Also well worth seeing is the town of Amasya. Founded by Amasis, Queen of the Amazons, on the banks of the River Yeşilırmak, it has royal tombs set into the cliff face. Turkish life at its most traditional thrives in the ancient commercial capital of Tokat, where painted horse-drawn carts bump along the cobbled streets and there are workshops housing textile printers, blacksmiths and saddlemakers.

Fasts and Festivals

Practically every month, there is a fair or festival being held somewhere in Turkey—from camel-wrestling fairs to more traditional displays of local culture and folklore. The most important annual religious event is Ramadan. The date of this 30-day-long fast is fixed according to the Muslim calendar, which is 11 days shorter than the Western one, and so it's timing varies from year to year. Strict fasting is observed between the hours of sunrise and sunset, and is broken each night with a hearty dinner that often turns into a social occasion with friends and neighbours. The end of Ramadan is marked by Şeker Bayrami, the Sugar Feast, when adults and children alike receive gifts of sweets.

Of equal importance in the Turkish calendar is *Kurban Bayrami*, the feast of sacrifice, which commemorates Abraham's willingness to sacrifice his son Isaac. Banks, offices, shops and factories close for several days, and people head to the countryside or the coast for a picnic. According to tradition, an animal, usually a lamb or a less expensive chicken—is offered as a sacrifice to mark the occasion.

If a line of cars, horns blaring, drives through a town or village, everyone knows that a circumcision ceremony is about to begin. In the villages the event is often marked with a procession, accompanied by a troupe of gypsy musicians. The boys taking part in the ceremony are between five and eleven years old and are dressed in splendidly colourful costumes. At the *Sünnet Düğünü* ("circumcision wedding") itself, a small cut marks the boys' entry into the adult world. As with a wedding feast, a circumcision is a momentous occasion, celebrated in the presence of many guests, and specialities such as wedding soup and wedding rice are typically served.

Tea, Coffee, Wine and *Rakı*

The Turks' favourite drink is *çay*, or black tea, which is drunk everywhere, and at any time of day. The most popular haunts for imbibing are the little *çayhane* or teahouses, which are traditionally a male domain.

The tea is prepared in two pots, stacked one on top of the other. Water is brought to the boil in the lower one, while the tea leaves are warmed through in the top one. Boiling water is then poured over the leaves, and the mixture is left to stand until the leaves settle. A little of the powerful brew is poured into a glass and diluted to taste with water from the lower pot. Apart from black tea, herb tea *(adaçayı)* and apple tea *(elmaçayı)* are also popular.

To make the famous sweet Turkish coffee—*kahve*—a heaped teaspoonful of finely ground arabica coffee, sugar to taste and 5 cl of water are placed in an individual copper or aluminium pot known as a *cezve*. The mixture is then brought to the boil three times and poured into a tiny cup.

Other favourite drinks are *ayran*—chilled yogurt whisked with water and a pinch of salt—and *salep*, made from the ground root of the salep orchid *(orchis mascula)*, hot milk, sugar and a pinch of cinnamon. *Salep* is a favourite cold remedy in wintertime.

Wine has a long tradition in Turkey. *Şarap*, as the Turks call wine, was being produced in Anatolia as long ago as 4,000 BC. Today, the three main growing areas (Eastern Thrace and Marmara, the Aegean coast, and central Anatolia) supply good quality red and white wines to suit every taste. A number of smaller vineyards are

found near Tokat, inland from the Black Sea, and in southeastern and eastern Anatolia. Grape varieties from different regions are often mixed; these include both native grapes and types imported from France during the 1930s. Among the pioneers of modern winemaking are the Doluca and Kavaklıdere wineries.

Rakı, a spirit that is distilled from grapes or—more rarely—figs, and flavoured with aniseed, is particularly appreciated in Turkey. Served on ice and diluted with water (which turns the mixture cloudy), it is drunk in tall, slender glasses, especially in the evening, as an accompaniment to *meze*, a selection of small, tasty appetizers. A meal like this is known as a *rakı sofrası*, or "*rakı* table".

Dressed in the traditional uniform of the Janissaries, or Sultan's guard, and accompanied by a marching band, these men make a splendid sight as they parade through the formal gardens of the sultan's palace.

Clad in their distinctive headscarfs, women inspect produce on sale at a stall in Ünye on the Black Sea; farmers in many areas make a living selling their crops at local markets.

SOUPS AND EGG DISHES

S oup (*çorba*) occupies a place of honour in Turkish cuisine, whether as a sustaining snack, or as a starter before the main course at the midday or evening meal. It forms the traditional breakfast in many rural areas, where every large village has its own *çorbacı*, or soup cook, who is in his kitchen early in the morning preparing great steaming pots of soup and freshly baked bread to accompany it. On market days, all the tables are quickly occupied by hungry shoppers eager for a bowl of the day's cheap and filling special. Soup, incidentally, is always "drunk"—the Turks never use the word "eat" in relation to soup.

Soup is often seasoned at the table with mint- or paprika-butter, garlic vinegar or lemon juice, and is always served with bread. One popular speciality is tripe soup, said to work wonders for those who have indulged in too much alcohol! There are even special tripe soup bars, which stay open until the small hours for the benefit of late-night revellers.

Nearly every rural family in Turkey owns some free-range hens, and eggs form part of the everyday diet. For breakfast, hard-boiled eggs are sliced and layered on fresh bread; and to make a quick, cheap snack—at any time of day—they are scrambled with vegetables, or fried with garlic sausage

and served in little individual frying pans. A particular summertime favourite is egg with yogurt sauce, which is scooped up with pieces of delicious flat bread.

Alpine soup

Not difficult · Central Anatolia

Yayla çorbası

Serves 4 to 6

80 g long-grain rice
1 large onion
60 g butter
1.5 litres beef stock
350 g whole milk plain yogurt
2 small eggs
1 rounded tbsp flour
2 tbsp lemon juice
salt
freshly ground black pepper
1½ tsp dried mint

Preparation time: 30 minutes
(plus 25 to 35 minutes' cooking time)

900 kJ/210 calories per portion (if serving 6)

1 Rinse and drain the rice in a sieve. Peel the onion and chop it into small pieces. Heat 30 g of the butter in a saucepan and sauté the chopped onion over medium heat until transparent. Add 1.25 litres of the stock and bring to the boil. Stir in the rice, cover and cook over low heat for 20 to 30 minutes, until the rice is tender.

2 Place the yogurt, eggs and flour in a bowl and stir with a hand whisk until smooth. Heat the remaining ¼ litre beef stock, then whisk it into the yogurt mixture. Remove the pan of rice from the heat and leave to cool briefly before stirring in the yogurt and egg mixture.

3 Heat the soup gently over medium heat, stirring constantly, until it begins to thicken. Do not let it boil, otherwise it will curdle. Add the lemon juice and season to taste with salt and pepper.

4 In a small frying pan, heat the rest of the butter until it froths, then stir in the mint. Stir the butter mixture into the soup, then pour into individual serving bowls. Serve at once with fresh *pide* (flat bread, *see page 65*) or some other freshly baked white bread.

Note: Turkish yogurt is fairly sour. If you are using very mild yogurt, add a little more lemon juice.

Yayla

The closest translation of the word *yayla* is "alpine pasture"—which may be a high, grassy plain, or an oasis of green in the mountains. In summer, Turkish families who make their living from livestock move with their flocks of sheep and goats to these cool, somewhat inaccessible pastures, where they will all live until the beginning of winter.

It is a fascinating sight to come across one of these caravans on its way to the mountains; the families' household goods, including copper cooking pots and bedding, are all loaded onto camels and horses or, as is more often the case today, onto lorries. Following nomadic tradition, the families live in tents made from dark goat's hair, and make their own butter and cheese. They also make the yogurt that forms the basis of the *yayla çorbası*, or alpine soup.

For the people living along Turkey's steamy Mediterranean coast, the *yayla* provides the perfect environment for a holiday. When the temperature reaches an unbearable 40 to 45°C, many elderly people, and women with babies and young children, move to their summer houses in the mountains, where the climate is pleasantly cool and there is plenty of water. Those who work during the week travel up at weekends. The women spend their time preserving the vegetables that grow here; the produce may be pickled, bottled, dried or made into paste to use throughout the winter.

27

Wedding soup

Düğün çorbası

Needs care • Central Anatolia

Serves 4

500 g veal or lamb, with bones
1 large onion
1 large carrot
1 bay leaf
salt
60 g butter
2 tbsp flour
2 eggs
juice of 1 lemon
freshly ground black pepper
1 tsp hot paprika

Preparation time: 30 minutes
(plus 1 hour's cooking time)

1,300 kJ/310 calories per portion

1 Rinse the meat under cold running water and place it in a saucepan. Peel and chop the vegetables, and add them to the meat with the bay leaf, a little salt and 1½ litres water.

2 Bring the water to the boil, cover the pan and cook over low heat for about 1 hour, skimming any scum from the surface as soon as it forms. Strain the soup through a colander.

3 Remove the meat from the bones, chop it into small cubes and set aside. Rub the vegetables through a fine sieve into the stock.

4 Heat 30 g of the butter in another saucepan. Stir in the flour with a hand whisk and brown briefly. Add the stock and bring to the boil, stirring. Remove the saucepan from the heat.

5 Whisk the eggs in a bowl with the lemon juice. Stir in a ladleful of the hot soup. Using a hand whisk, stir the egg mixture into the soup and heat through gently until it thickens. Do not let it boil, otherwise it will curdle.

6 Season the soup to taste with salt and pepper. Add the chopped meat. In a small frying pan, heat the remaining butter and stir in the paprika. Pour the soup into individual bowls. At the table, drizzle a little seasoned butter over each portion of soup. Serve with fresh *pide* (flat bread, *see page 65*).

Green pea soup

Bezelye çorbası

Not difficult • Aegean coast

Serves 4 to 6

2 medium-sized onions
1 lettuce
1 bunch flat-leaf parsley
300 g young frozen peas
60 g butter
1½ litres chicken stock
1 tbsp lemon juice
salt
freshly ground black pepper
2 slices white bread
½ tsp mild or hot paprika

Preparation time: 30 minutes
(plus 25 minutes' cooking time)

690 kJ/160 calories per portion
(if serving 6)

1 Peel and finely chop the onions. Remove any damaged leaves from the lettuce. Separate the lettuce leaves, wash and shake dry, then cut them into strips. Wash the parsley, shake dry, and coarsely chop the leaves. Remove the peas from the freezer.

2 Heat half the butter in a saucepan. Add the onions, lettuce, parsley and 200 g of the frozen peas, and toss over medium heat for about 5 minutes. Add the chicken stock, cover and cook for about 20 minutes.

3 Rub the soup through a fine sieve into a second saucepan. Add the rest of the peas and cook for about 5 minutes.

Add the lemon juice and season to taste with salt and pepper.

4 Cut the bread into 1 cm dice. Heat the remaining butter in a frying pan and fry the bread cubes until crisp, then sprinkle with the paprika.

5 Pour the soup into individual bowls and scatter the croûtons over the top.

Note: To add a distinctive flavour, chop a few leaves of fresh mint and sprinkle them over the soup.

Red lentil soup

Not difficult • Southeastern Anatolia

Kırmızı mercimek çorbası

Serves 4 to 6

250 g red lentils
1 large onion
1 large carrot
80 g butter
1.25 litres vegetable stock
¼ litre milk
1 tbsp lemon juice
salt
freshly ground black pepper
3 slices white bread
1 tsp hot or mild paprika

Preparation time: 30 minutes
(plus 30 minutes' cooking time)

1,300 kJ/310 calories per portion
(if serving 6)

1 Place the lentils in a sieve, removing any small stones, rinse them under cold running water and drain well. Peel and finely chop the onion and carrot.

2 Heat 20 g of the butter in a saucepan and sauté the onion until transparent. Add the carrot and sauté for 5 minutes. Stir in the stock and the drained lentils, bring to the boil and cook over low heat for about 30 minutes, stirring the soup from time to time.

3 Rub the lentils and the vegetables through a fine sieve into a second pan. Stir in the milk and return the soup to the boil. Add the lemon juice and season to taste with salt and pepper.

4 Cut the bread into 1 cm cubes. Heat 30 g butter in a frying pan and fry the croûtons until crisp.

5 Heat the remaining butter in a small frying pan and stir in the paprika. Pour the soup into individual bowls. At the table, add paprika butter and some croûtons to each portion. Serve with fresh *pide* (flat bread, *see page 65*).

Note: The soup thickens if it is left to stand. To thin it, add stock or milk.

Lentils

Lentils come in different sizes and colours—red, yellow, green and brown. Among the Turks' favourite pulses are red lentils (which change from orangy-red to dull yellow during cooking). Native to the Middle East, they have been cultivated in Turkey since about 7000 BC. Today, the main growing area is near the town of Sanliurfa in southeast Anatolia, close to the Euphrates River and its tributaries. Here, the region's dry, hot summers provide the ideal conditions for cultivating these leguminous plants.

Lentils are very good for making hearty soups, popular throughout Turkey. In addition, there is a whole range of regional dishes, such as lentil croquettes *(mercimek köftesi)*, a speciality of Gaziantep in southeastern Anatolia. Flat green lentils are also widely eaten—cooked with minced meat and tomatoes, for example—but they are not as popular as the red ones.

Like all members of the pulse family, lentils are a highly valuable source of protein and minerals, including iron, calcium and phosphorus, as well as vitamin B and niacin. They do not need soaking before cooking, but it is a good idea to place them in a sieve and pick them over to remove any small stones, before rinsing well under cold running water.

Ezo, the bride's soup

Ezo gelin çorbası

Not difficult • Mediterranean coast

Serves 4 to 6

100 g red lentils
100 g finely ground burghul
(cracked wheat)
1 large onion
60 g butter
2 tbsp tomato purée
1 tsp hot paprika purée or sambal
ulek (see Glossary)
salt • freshly ground black pepper
1 tsp dried mint
2 sprigs fresh mint or flat-leaf
parsley

Preparation time: 30 minutes
(plus 45 minutes' cooking time)

790 kJ/190 calories per portion
(if serving 6)

1 Place the lentils in a sieve, removing any stones, then rinse them under cold running water and drain. Place the burghul in a sieve, rinse it under cold running water and then drain. Peel and finely chop the onion.

2 Heat 30 g of the butter in a saucepan and sauté the onion until transparent. Add 1.5 litres water and stir in the lentils and burghul. Stir the tomato purée with ¼ litre water until smooth, then add it to the pan. Cook the soup over low heat for about 45 minutes, stirring from time to time.

3 Rub the soup through a fine sieve into a second pan. If it is too thick, add a little more water. Return the soup to the boil and add the paprika purée or *sambal ulek* and season generously with salt and pepper.

4 Heat the rest of the butter in a small frying pan. Stir in the dried mint, then stir the mint butter into the soup. Wash the fresh mint or parsley and shake dry. Chop the leaves and sprinkle them over the soup before serving.

Note: A few sliced mushrooms can be added to give extra interest to the soup. Stir them in about 10 minutes before the end of the cooking time.

Tripe soup

İşkembe çorbası

More complicated • Istanbul

Serves 4 to 6

300 g veal or mutton tripe, ready-
cooked by the butcher
salt
60 g butter
1½ tbsp plain flour
2 egg yolks
juice of ½ lemon
1 tsp hot paprika
2 garlic cloves
5 cl white wine vinegar

Preparation time: 30 minutes
(plus 20 minutes' cooking time)

630 kJ/150 calories per portion
(if serving 6)

1 Rinse the tripe thoroughly under cold running water and cut it into very thin strips about 2.5 cm long. Place the strips in a saucepan with 1 litre salted water, cover and cook over low heat for about 20 minutes. Remove the tripe from the stock with a slotted spoon and reserve the stock.

2 Heat 30 g of the butter in a second pan. Stir in the flour and cook until lightly browned. Stir in half the stock, a little at a time, and simmer gently. Add the rest of the stock and the tripe, then return the soup to the boil and cook over low heat for about 3 minutes.

3 Whisk the egg yolks with the lemon juice. Allow the soup to cool briefly, then stir in the egg mixture. Heat through gently until the soup thickens, but do not allow it to boil, otherwise it will curdle. Season lightly with salt.

4 Heat the remaining butter and stir in the paprika. Peel the garlic and crush it with salt in a mortar. Stir in the vinegar and 5 cl water. Pour the soup into individual bowls and add a little of the paprika butter to each portion. Guests can then season the soup to taste with 1 to 2 tbsp garlic vinegar. Serve with fresh *pide* (flat bread, *see page 65*).

Tarhana soup

Tarhana çorbası

Fairly easy • Central Anatolia

Serves 4 to 6

3 long, pointed sweet peppers (see Glossary)
3 medium-sized tomatoes
2 garlic cloves
30 g butter
200 g minced beef or lamb
100 g tarhana (soup base • see below)
1 tbsp tomato purée
½ tsp mild or hot paprika
salt
freshly ground black pepper
15 g flat-leaf parsley

Preparation time: 30 minutes (plus 15 minutes' cooking time)

810 kJ/190 calories per portion (if serving 6)

1 Wash the sweet peppers and halve them lengthwise. Remove the stalks, seeds and white ribs. Rinse the peppers and cut them into small pieces.

2 Plunge the tomatoes into boiling water and allow them to stand briefly. Remove the skins, then chop the flesh. Peel and finely chop the garlic.

3 Heat the butter in a saucepan and sauté the garlic until transparent, then add the meat. Using a spoon, crumble the meat, then stir-fry it over high heat until all the juices have evaporated and it is lightly browned. Stir in the peppers and tomatoes, and continue to fry over

medium heat for about 2 minutes. Pour in 1.25 litres water, stir well and bring the soup to the boil.

4 Mix the *tarhana* and tomato purée with ¼ litre water. Stir until smooth then stir the mixture into the soup. Cover the pan and simmer over low heat for about 15 minutes, stirring from time to time so that the soup does not stick to the pan.

5 Stir in the paprika and season to taste with salt and pepper. Wash the parsley and shake dry. Chop the leaves and sprinkle them over the soup just before serving it.

Tarhana

This soup base was invented by the ancient nomadic Turkish tribes of central Asia, for whom it was a way of using yogurt to make a nourishing food that would also keep well. As these tribes advanced westwards, so modern nomads brought their food preserving traditions with them, and continued to practise them even when they settled permanently.

Tarhana is made from cooked, dried and crushed wheat mixed with yogurt and cooked to a dough. This dough is drained, and seasoned with salt, pepper, paprika and tomatoes; it may also be enriched with onions and stock. It is then pressed through a very fine sieve, crumbled wih the

fingers to make granules or small sticks, and left out in the sun to dry.

An alternative way to make *tarhana* is to knead flour and yogurt together, then leave it to stand for a few days so that it goes sour. The dough is then cut into cubes, dried and grated.

Although Turkish cooks still make their own supplies of *tarhana*—often

with additional flavourings such as cherry, beetroot juice or mint—it is now produced industrially. Today, the majority of the commercially mass-produced *tarhana* is exported.

In the UK, *tarhana* is sold in Greek and Middle Eastern food shops. It stores well and can be used to add a delicately tart flavour to soups.

Eggs with vegetables

Quick • Aegean coast   **Menemen**   *Serves 4*

1 bunch spring onions
4 medium-sized tomatoes
4 hot or mild green chili peppers
(see Glossary)
50 g butter
6 eggs
salt
freshly ground black pepper
15 g flat-leaf parsley

Preparation time: 30 minutes

980 kJ/230 calories
per portion

1 Wash and trim the spring onions, and cut the white parts into thin rings (only the white parts are used).

2 Plunge the tomatoes into boiling water and allow them to stand briefly. Remove the skins, then chop the flesh.

3 Wash the chili peppers, cut them in half lengthwise and remove the stalks. Rinse the chili halves and cut them crosswise into thin strips.

4 Heat the butter in a large frying pan and sauté the spring onion rings until transparent, then add the tomatoes and chili peppers, and stir-fry over medium heat for 4 to 5 minutes.

5 Break the eggs into a bowl, whisk with a little salt, then pour them over the vegetables. Very gently stir the eggs and vegetables with a spatula until they begin to set. *Menemen* should have a moist consistency. Season to taste with salt and pepper.

6 Wash the parsley and shake it dry. Finely chop the leaves and sprinkle them over the scrambled eggs. Serve at once with fresh *pide* (flat bread, *see page 65*).

Note: In Turkey, *menemen* is always cooked and served in small, individual, aluminium frying pans.

Poached eggs in yogurt sauce

Easy • Aegean coast Çılbır *Serves 4 (main course) or 8 (starter)*

700 g whole milk plain yogurt
4 garlic cloves
salt
1 tsp hot paprika
4 tbsp sunflower oil
12.5 cl white wine vinegar
8 eggs

Preparation time: 30 minutes

820 kJ/200 calories per portion
(if serving 8)

1 Pour the yogurt into a bowl. Peel and crush the garlic, and stir into the bowl of yogurt. Add a little salt and stir well. In a separate bowl, stir the paprika into the sunflower oil.

2 Bring 2 litres water to the boil in a wide saucepan. Add the vinegar and return the water to the boil. Break the eggs, one at a time, into a ladle and slide each one into the boiling water. Reduce the heat. Place a lid on the pan and poach the eggs for 4 to 6 minutes, until the whites are firm. Remove the lid. Using a slotted spoon, scoop the eggs out of the water and dip them

briefly in a bowl of cold water. Remove them from the bowl with the slotted spoon and drain off the water. Arrange the poached eggs on a serving dish.

3 Pour the yogurt sauce over the eggs. Drizzle the paprika and oil over the yogurt. Serve the eggs with fresh *pide* (flat bread, *see page 65*), if liked.

Note: Poached eggs in yogurt sauce make a delicious light summer meal, but are also suitable as a starter. Serve the eggs as soon as they are cooked, while their yolks are still warm.

STARTERS AND SALADS

First-time visitors to Turkey are often overwhelmed when the waiter in a restaurant arrives bearing a huge tray covered with small dishes of hors d'œuvres. Among the delights on offer will be salads, served with or without yogurt, puréed, stuffed, fried, pickled or boiled vegetables, succulent morsels of fish, spicy pieces of liver, cheese or lentil dips, and crisp pastry rolls. There may also be simpler fare such as shredded carrot and cucumber, ewe's milk cheese, plump olives and crunchy salad leaves. Diners who fail to keep a tight rein on themselves may find they do not have room for the main course!

But that is what a "*rakı* table", as this display of culinary bravura is called, is all about, and nothing whets the appetite more than savouring a selection of such exquisite and varied titbits in the company of friends. To accompany the feast there is always plenty of fresh white bread—indispensable at any meal in Turkey—as well as glasses of wine or the potent, aniseed-flavoured spirit *rakı* which gives this way of eating its name.

Turkey has a wide variety of cold vegetable dishes, small pastries, fish and meat dishes suitable for serving as starters. At family meals, two or three little appetizers or salads are common, and even more are served on special occasions, or when guests are present.

Cucumber salad with yogurt

Quick • Central Anatolia   **Cacık**   *Serves 4*

1 large cucumber
700 g whole-milk plain yogurt
2 garlic cloves
15 g dill
salt
2 tsp virgin olive oil
1 tsp dried mint

Preparation time: 20 minutes

610 kJ/150 calories per portion

1 Peel the cucumber and cut it in half lengthwise. Scrape out the seeds with a teaspoon. Cut the cucumber into small dice. Whisk the yogurt in a bowl with ¼ litre ice-cold water.

2 Peel and crush the garlic, and stir it into the yogurt and water. Wash the dill and shake it dry. Finely chop the leaves and add them to the ingredients in the bowl.

3 Sprinkle a little salt over the yogurt mixture, add the diced cucumber and stir thoroughly to mix the ingredients.

4 Serve the *cacık* in individual bowls or on small plates and drizzle ½ tsp olive oil over each portion. Sprinkle with a little mint before serving.

Note: In Turkey, *cacık* is eaten as a starter or a between-meals snack. It is especially refreshing when served chilled. It can either be chilled in the refrigerator before serving or, instead of water, an equivalent quantity of ice cubes can be added to the yogurt.

Shepherd's salad

Çoban salatası

Easy • Coastal regions

Serves 4

1 bunch spring onions
4 medium-sized tomatoes
1 medium-sized cucumber
3 mild or hot green chili peppers
(see Glossary)
30 g flat-leaf parsley
2 tbsp virgin olive oil
2 tbsp white wine vinegar or lemon
juice
salt
freshly ground black pepper
50 g black olives
1 unwaxed lemon

Preparation time: 20 minutes

550 kJ/130 calories per portion

1 Wash and trim the spring onions and cut them into rings. Wash and halve the tomatoes, and chop the flesh into 1 cm dice. Peel the cucumber and cut it into 1 cm dice. Arrange all the ingredients on a serving dish.

2 Wash the chili peppers and discard the stalks. Cut the peppers into rings. If you prefer a less fiery flavour, halve the chili peppers lengthwise, removing the seeds and ribs, and cut them into small, thin strips.

3 Wash the parsley and shake it dry. Finely chop the leaves, then sprinkle them, together with the chili peppers, over the vegetables on the dish.

4 Mix together the oil and vinegar or lemon juice to make a dressing, and season to taste with salt and pepper. Drizzle the dressing over the salad.

5 Rinse the olives under cold running water, pat them dry and sprinkle them over the salad. Wash the lemon in hot water and cut it into eight wedges. Arrange the wedges around the edge of the plate, so that everyone can season the salad with lemon juice to taste.

Note: The salad can also be topped with crumbled ewe's milk cheese or coarsely grated radishes. In winter, you can add coarsely grated carrots or finely shredded red cabbage.

Pink princess salad

Pembe sultan salatası

Simple • Black Sea coast

Serves 4 to 6

800 g beetroot
525 g whole milk plain yogurt
3 garlic cloves
salt
2 to 3 tbsp lemon juice
30 g flat-leaf parsley

Preparation time: 45 minutes
(plus 1 to 1½ hours' cooking time,
plus cooling time)

470 kJ/110 calories per portion
(if serving 6)

1 Wash the beetroot and place in a saucepan with enough water to cover. Cook over medium heat, covered, for 1 to 1½ hours, depending on the size of the beetroot. They are ready when they can be pierced easily with a fork.

2 Meanwhile, suspend a conical sieve over a bowl and line it with a coffee filter bag. Pour in the yogurt and leave it to drain for about 20 minutes.

3 Transfer the beetroot to a colander and rinse them under cold running water. Leave to cool before peeling, then grate them into a bowl.

4 Add the strained yogurt to the beetroot. Peel and crush the garlic, and stir it into the beetroot mixture. Add salt and lemon juice to taste. Stir thoroughly and adjust the seasoning, if necessary.

5 Wash the parsley and shake it dry. Tear off the leaves and use them to garnish the salad.

Variation: Carrot salad

(Yoğurtlu havuc ezmesi)
This can be prepared in exactly the same way. Coarsely grate 800 g peeled carrots and stir-fry in 3 to 4 tbsp olive oil over medium heat for 10 minutes. Leave the carrots to cool and then mix with 525 g strained yogurt, 2 crushed garlic cloves, and salt and lemon juice to taste.

Purslane in yogurt sauce

Yoğurtlu semizotu

Easy • Aegean coast

Serves 4

350 g whole milk plain yogurt
600 g purslane (see Note)
2 tbsp mayonnaise
salt
2 tbsp lemon juice
3 garlic cloves
4 lemon slices, halved, for garnish

Preparation time: 30 minutes

640 kJ/150 calories per portion

1 Suspend a conical sieve over a large bowl and line it with a coffee filter bag. Pour in the yogurt and leave it to drain for about 20 minutes.

2 Meanwhile, wash and drain the purslane. Discard the roots and tough stalks. Coarsely chop the leaves and the tender stalks.

3 Mix the yogurt with the mayonnaise, salt and lemon juice. Peel and crush the garlic, and stir it into the yogurt. Stir the chopped purslane into the yogurt sauce, adjust the seasoning and serve at once, garnished with the halved lemon slices.

Note: Purslane is a small plant with reddish stems and thick, fleshy, rounded leaves. It has a sour, nutty flavour and is rich in minerals, vitamins A and C, and B group vitamins. A great favourite with the Turks, it is unfortunately rarely sold in Britain. However, it is easy to grow in the garden in early summer, though you need to plant plenty of seeds to grow enough for a salad. It can be picked after three or four weeks, or even sooner if grown under glass or plastic. Purslane can also be served warm, sautéed with onions and minced meat.

Courgette fritters

Mücver

Takes time • Istanbul

Serves 4

800 g courgettes, preferably small, firm ones
salt
3 spring onions
30 g dill
30 g flat-leaf parsley
3 tbsp plain flour
2 tbsp freshly-grated kaşar (or emmenthal) cheese
3 eggs
10 cl sunflower oil for frying

Preparation time: 1 hour

700 kJ/170 calories per portion

1 Wash the courgettes, top-and-tail them and trim off any damaged parts with a sharp knife. Coarsely grate the courgettes, mix with salt and leave to stand for about 15 minutes to draw off the bitter juice.

2 Wash and trim the spring onions and cut them into very thin rings. Wash the dill and parsley, shake dry and finely chop the leaves.

3 Transfer the grated courgettes to a fine sieve and squeeze out the juice. Mix the courgettes with the spring onions, herbs, flour, grated cheese and eggs, and stir thoroughly. Season to taste with salt.

4 Heat 2 to 3 tbsp oil in a frying pan. Drop a few tablespoonsful of the mixture at a time into the pan, gently press flat and fry over medium heat for 2 to 3 minutes on each side, until the fritters are golden-brown. Drain on paper towels and keep warm. Prepare all the fritters in the same way and then serve hot.

Drink: *Rakı*, diluted with iced water, or well-chilled dry white wine such as Kavaklıdere Primeur from Cappadocia, goes well with this dish.

Herby cheese dip

Haydari

Easy • Mediterranean coast

Serves 4 to 6

700 g whole milk plain yogurt
200 g beyaz peynir (ewe's milk cheese • see page 71)
15 g flat-leaf parsley
15 g dill
15 g mint
2 garlic cloves
1 tbsp lemon juice
2 hot red chili peppers (see Glossary)
50 g black olives

Preparation time: 30 minutes (plus chilling time)

790 kJ/190 calories per portion (if serving 6)

1 Suspend a conical sieve over a bowl and line it with a coffee filter bag, then pour in the yogurt and leave it to drain for about 20 minutes.

2 Meanwhile, using a fork, very finely mash the cheese in a bowl. Wash the herbs, shake them dry and very finely chop the leaves. Add the herbs to the cheese. Peel and crush the garlic, and stir it into the cheese. Stir thoroughly.

3 Add the strained yogurt and lemon juice to the cheese mixture and stir until it forms a smooth paste. Leave the herby cheese dip to chill in the refrigerator for about 1 hour.

4 Wash the chili peppers, discarding the stalks, and chop the flesh into rings. If you prefer a less fiery flavour, halve the chili peppers lengthwise, removing the seeds and ribs, and cut them into small, thin strips.

5 Rinse the olives under cold running water and pat them dry. Transfer the chilled *haydari* to a small serving dish and serve it garnished with the chili peppers and olives.

Burghul salad

Quick • Central Anatolia

Kısır

Serves 4 to 6

200 g burghul (cracked wheat)
3 medium-sized tomatoes
1 bunch spring onions
4 hot or mild green chili peppers (see Glossary)
30 g flat-leaf parsley
15 g mint
1 tbsp tomato purée
3 tbsp virgin olive oil
juice of 1 lemon
1 tsp mild paprika
ground cumin
freshly ground black pepper • salt

Preparation time: 30 minutes (plus 30 minutes for soaking the burghul)

680 kJ/160 calories per portion (if serving 6)

1 Place the burghul in a bowl and stir in 30 cl lukewarm water. Leave it to soak for about 30 minutes, until all the water has been absorbed.

2 Meanwhile, wash the vegetables. Halve the tomatoes and chop the flesh very finely. Wash and trim the spring onions and cut them into thin rings. Cut the chili peppers in half lengthwise and remove the stalks and seeds. Rinse the chili peppers and cut them into very thin shreds.

3 Wash the parsley and mint, shake dry and finely chop the leaves. Mix the tomato purée, olive oil, lemon juice, paprika and a little cumin, pepper and salt together, then stir the mixture into the burghul. Add the chopped herbs

and vegetables, and fold them into the burghul. Leave the salad to stand for about 10 minutes. If necessary, adjust the seasoning before serving.

Drink: *Rakı*, diluted with iced water, is an excellent choice to serve with this refreshing salad.

Note: Small quantities of *kısır* can be served on the small, tender leaves of the heart of a cos lettuce and then eaten with the fingers.

Aubergine salad

Not difficult • Coastal regions

Patlıcan salatası

Serves 4 to 6

800 g small aubergines
juice of 1 lemon
2 garlic cloves
3 tbsp virgin olive oil
salt
2 medium-sized tomatoes
50 g black olives

Preparation time: 30 minutes (plus 25 to 30 minutes' cooking time)

470 kJ/110 calories per portion (if serving 6)

1 Preheat the oven to 250° (450°F or Mark 8). Wash the aubergines and peel away the green leaves around the stalks, but do not remove the stalks.

2 Pierce the aubergines several times with a fork, then place in a roasting pan and bake in the centre of the oven for 25 to 30 minutes, until they are tender. Peel the aubergines while they are still hot, holding them by the stalk, then cut off the stalks. Sprinkle the aubergines at once with lemon juice.

3 Place the aubergines on a chopping board and chop them very finely with a large knife, to create a purée-like

consistency. Transfer the aubergine purée to a bowl. Peel the garlic cloves, cut them into pieces, then crush them, using a pestle and mortar. Stir in the olive oil, then stir the mixture into the aubergine purée. Season with salt.

4 Place the salad in the refrigerator. Just before serving, wash the tomatoes and cut them into eighths. Rinse the olives under cold running water and pat them dry. Garnish the salad with a pattern of tomatoes and olives.

Note: If using large aubergines for this dish, carefully scrape out the seeds before chopping the flesh.

Chick-pea purée

Hummus

Serves 6

200 g dried chick-peas
juice of 2 lemons
3 garlic cloves
120 g tahini (sesame paste)
ground cumin
salt
30 g flat-leaf parsley
4 tbsp virgin olive oil
1 tsp hot paprika

Preparation time: 40 minutes (plus 12 hours for soaking the chick-peas and 50 minutes' cooking time)

1,200 kJ/290 calories per portion

1 Place the chick-peas in a sieve, rinse them under cold running water, and leave them to soak overnight in plenty of water. Transfer them to a saucepan with enough water to cover, bring to the boil and boil vigorously for 10 minutes. Skim the scum from the surface, cover and cook over low heat for about 50 minutes, until tender.

2 Rinse the chick-peas briefly under cold, running water, then skin them by rubbing each chick-pea between your thumb and index finger.

3 Purée the skinned chick-peas in a food processor, then rub them through a fine sieve. Stir in the lemon juice. Peel and crush the garlic, and stir it into the purée.

4 Stir the *tahini* thoroughly so that the solids and oil are well blended, then stir the required quantity into the purée. Season with a little cumin and salt. Wash the parsley, shake it dry, then chop the leaves very finely and stir them into the *hummus*, mixing thoroughly. If the *hummus* is too thick, add 2 to 3 tbsp cold water.

5 Transfer the *hummus* to a serving dish. Mix the olive oil with the paprika and drizzle over the top. Serve with freshly baked *pide* (flat bread, *see page 65*).

Note: For a cocktail snack, spread a little *hummus* on small slices of white bread, and garnish with a little chopped parsley or strips of sweet pepper.

Sesame seeds and tahini

The sesame plant (*susam* in Turkish) was being cultivated in eastern Anatolia at the time of the Urartian empire (900-700 BC). Today, it is found mainly in the Mediterranean region and southeastern Anatolia. The black or white edible seeds, which are harvested during July and August, contain 50 per cent oil and a number of vitamins. They are also reputed to be an aphrodisiac.

Whole or ground, sesame seeds have a wide range of uses in Turkish cuisine. They are sprinkled whole on breads and pastries before baking to give an added nutty flavour; and they are crushed and mixed with sugar and aromatics to make the delicious, rich sweetmeat known as *halva*. Sold in blocks, *halva* is eaten sliced, sprinkled with a little lemon juice, and served with a glass of water to take the edge off the sweetness.

To make *tahini*—a thick, oily paste that is an essential ingredient in many of the small savoury dishes known as *meze*—the seeds are ground very finely. In mountain villages, this paste is still produced in primitive grain mills beside the streams. For a snack, the Turks like to dip bread in a mixture of *tahini* and *pekmez*, a syrup made from grapes, and they also use *tahini* in salad dressings.

If *tahini* is left to stand, the solids and oil will separate, so it must be stirred before use. It should not be kept for long, as it turns rancid.

Bean salad

Takes time • Mediterranean coast

Taratorlu piyaz

Serves 4 to 6

250 g small, dried white beans
2 medium-sized tomatoes
2 medium-sized red onions
2 mild green chili peppers (see Glossary)
4 to 5 tbsp red wine vinegar
4 tbsp virgin olive oil
salt • freshly ground black pepper
4 tbsp tahini (sesame paste)
juice of ½ lemon
2 hard-boiled eggs
50 g black olives
30 g flat-leaf parsley

Preparation time: 45 minutes
(plus 12 hours for soaking the beans
and 35 to 45 minutes' cooking time)

1,100 kJ/260 calories per portion
(if serving 6)

1 Wash the white beans and soak them overnight in plenty of cold water. In fresh water, bring the beans to the boil and boil for 10 minutes. Skim the scum from the surface, cover and cook over low heat for 35 to 45 minutes. The beans should not be allowed to burst while cooking. Leave them to cool, preferably in the cooking water.

2 Wash the tomatoes, cut them in half and chop the flesh. Peel the onions, cut them into quarters and slice thinly. Wash the chili peppers and cut in half lengthwise, discarding the stalks and seeds. Rinse, then cut into thin strips.

3 Strain the cooled beans through a sieve and allow to drain, then divide them between four or six individual bowls or soup plates. To make the dressing, mix the vinegar, oil and salt and pepper and drizzle the mixture over the beans. Sprinkle each portion with some of the prepared vegetables.

4 Stir the *tahini* thoroughly so that the solids and oil are well blended, then mix the required quantity in a bowl with the lemon juice, salt and 5 tbsp water. Spoon 2 to 3 tbsp of the sesame dressing over each portion of salad. Shell the eggs and cut them into four. Rinse the olives under cold running water and pat them dry. Wash the parsley, shake it dry, and finely chop the leaves. Garnish each portion of beans attractively with egg, parsley and olives. Serve with white bread or *pide* (flat bread, *see page 65*).

Fried aubergines

Easy • Coastal regions

Patlıcan kızartması

Serves 4

500 g aubergines
salt
8 mild or hot green chili peppers (see Glossary)
3 tbsp plain flour
10 cl olive oil for frying
525 g whole milk plain yogurt
3 garlic cloves

Preparation time: 30 minutes
(plus 15 minutes' standing time)

730 kJ/170 calories per portion

1 Remove the aubergine stalks, then wash the aubergines and cut them lengthwise into slices about 5 mm thick. Sprinkle lightly with salt and leave to stand for about 15 minutes.

2 Wash the chili peppers and pat them dry. Sift the flour on to a flat plate. Pat the aubergine slices with paper towels to remove the moisture, then coat them with flour on both sides. Shake off any excess flour.

3 Heat enough oil in a frying pan to cover the base, then fry the aubergine slices, in batches, over high heat for 4 to 5 minutes, until golden-brown on both sides. Drain on paper towels. Fry the chili peppers whole, including the stalks, for 3 to 5 minutes, until brown all over, then drain off the fat.

4 Pour the yogurt into a bowl. Peel and crush the garlic, then stir it into the yogurt. Season to taste with salt and then stir the mixture thoroughly. Arrange the vegetables on a serving dish. Top with the yogurt and serve warm or cold.

Variation: Cut 500 g courgettes and parboiled carrots lengthwise into slices about 5 mm thick, and fry them. Serve with garlic-flavoured yogurt.

Circassian chicken

Çerkez tavuğu

Serves 6

1 oven-ready chicken (about 1.2 kg)
1 tsp black peppercorns
salt
1 medium-sized carrot
1 medium-sized onion
300 g shelled walnuts
½ tsp each mild and hot paprika
6 slices white bread
¼ litre milk
freshly ground black pepper
4 tbsp walnut oil
cayenne pepper
15 g flat-leaf parsley

Preparation time: 1 hour
(plus 1 hour's cooking time and
30 minutes' standing time)

3,100 kJ/740 calories per portion

1 Rinse the chicken inside and out, then place it in a fireproof casserole or saucepan with enough water to cover. Add the peppercorns and sprinkle with salt. Peel and chop the carrot and the onion and add them to the casserole. Bring to the boil, skim the scum from the surface, then cover and cook over low heat for 1 hour. Remove the chicken and leave it to cool. Reserve the stock.

2 Reserve eight of the walnut halves and grind the rest very finely in a food processor. Mix the ground walnuts in a saucepan with both the mild and the hot paprika, then toast them over medium heat for about 5 minutes *(above)*, stirring constantly, to sweat out the oil, then leave to cool.

3 Remove the crusts from the bread. Measure out ¼ litre of the reserved chicken stock, soak the bread in it, then squeeze gently. Mash the bread very finely with a fork, then add to the walnuts, together with the milk, and stir to a thick paste. Detach the meat from the breast and legs of the chicken. (Save the rest of the meat and stock to make soup.)

4 Cut the meat into several pieces, then tear it into fine shreds with your fingers *(above)*. Place the shreds in a bowl, and season with salt and a little pepper, then stir in half the walnut paste. Transfer half the mixture to a serving dish and smooth the surface. Mix the walnut oil with a little cayenne pepper. Sprinkle half this seasoned oil over the chicken and walnut mixture in the serving dish.

5 Spread 3 tbsp of the remaining walnut paste over the meat in the dish *(above)*, then cover with the remaining meat and walnut mixture. Spread the rest of the walnut paste on top, then sprinkle with the remaining walnut oil.

6 Wash the parsley, shake it dry, and tear off the leaves. Garnish the chicken with the parsley and the eight reserved walnut halves. Leave the mixture to stand at room temperature for about 30 minutes before serving.

Pickled peppers

Prepare in advance • Antalya

Biber turşusu

2.5 kg dolmalık biber (round, thin-skinned sweet peppers)
30 g mint
10 garlic cloves
1 very fresh, clean egg
about 500 g salt
about 70 cl red wine vinegar
1 heaped tsp citric acid (see Glossary)
1 tsp sugar
1 tbsp canned chick-peas

Preparation time: 45 minutes (plus 4 to 5 days' standing time)

89 kJ/21 calories per 100 g of pickles

1 Clean one 4-litre screw- or clip-top preserving jar or two 2-litre jars. Wash the peppers and mint, and drain them in a colander. Lay half the mint sprigs in the bottom of the jar. Using a sharp knife, make a cross-shaped incision about 1 cm deep in the rounded end of each pepper, directly opposite the stalk. Peel the garlic, then arrange the peppers and garlic in alternate layers in the jar.

2 Pour 3 litres of water into a large bowl and place the egg in the water. Pour the salt, a little at a time, into the water, stirring constantly until it dissolves. When the egg floats to the surface, the water is sufficiently salted. Remove the egg from the water.

3 Add the vinegar to the jar then top up with salted water until the jar is almost full. Add the citric acid, sugar and chick-peas. Rotate the jar back and forth to distribute the ingredients. Lay the rest of the mint on top.

4 Depending on the size of the jar, place a cup or china plate inside the jar on top of the ingredients to weigh them down. Put the lid on the jar and leave it in a cool, dark place. The peppers are ready to eat after 4 to 5 days, but they will keep for several months.

Note: To eat, pull off strips, starting at the cross-shaped incision at the base. Discard the core and stalk.

Pickles

During the reign of Mehmet II, the man who conquered Constantinople in 1453, the palace kitchen staff included a specialist cook whose sole job was making *turşu*—pickles. Since this time, the Turks have turned the pickling of vegetables and fruit into a real art form. Although the specialist *turşu* shops are sadly slowly dying out (one of the best still remains in Istanbul's Cihangir district), the *turşu* seller's cart is still a familiar sight on the streets of Turkey's larger towns and cities.

Many kinds of vegetables are preserved—either singly or mixed, in salt water or a mixture of salt water and vinegar—including baby marrows, cucumbers, sweetcorn, peppers, carrots and beans. Plums, pears, quinces and cherries are also suitable for preserving. The visual aspect is an important one, and among the more interesting pickles on sale are red and green sweet peppers and baby aubergines stuffed with shredded cabbage and wrapped in celery stalks. Pickles are made in great quantities during the summer months, when vegetables are cheap and plentiful.

These delicious sour pickles accompany both hot and cold dishes and salads, and are an essential ingredient in various appetizers; on the Black Sea coast, pickled white cabbage, sometimes sautéed with garlic, is a great favourite. The liquid in which the vegetables or fruit are preserved is not wasted either, for it is a popular drink.

GRAINS, PASTA, BREAD AND PASTRY

A pile of steaming rice *(pilav)*, topped with a few chick-peas or white beans, makes the simplest and cheapest of meals, equally popular in Turkey with rich and poor. Served with a glass of *ayran*, yogurt whisked with water, it is standard fare in cheaper restaurants.

Rice *(pirinç)* is one of the basic ingredients in Turkish cuisine; it is usually lightly fried with a little butter, then boiled in salted water. For added variety, slices of aubergine, almonds, grated carrots, rice-shaped pasta or offal may be cooked with the rice, as, for example, with *iç pilav*, festival rice.

Dishes such as *pilav* can just as equally well be made with bulghur wheat. Turkey produces its own cereal crops, which are grown mainly in the south and around the delta regions of the Ceyhan and Seyhan rivers. This chapter includes a whole range of dishes which can be prepared from a few staple ingredients. They include *börek* (flaky pastry with various fillings), pies and pastries made from phyllo or pasta dough, and the much-loved *mantı*, a type of ravioli.

No Turkish meal is complete without hunks of freshly baked bread. Paper-thin flat bread is traditionally prepared by Turkish cooks at home, the results every bit as good as those produced by the village baker.

Festival rice

Not difficult · Istanbul   İç pilav

250 g long-grain rice
50 g very small currants (kuş üzümü)
1 medium-sized onion
200 g lamb's liver
50 g butter
50 g pine nuts
¾ litre chicken stock
¼ tsp ground allspice
freshly ground black pepper
ground cinnamon
ground cumin
15 g dill
salt

Preparation time: 30 minutes
(plus 25 minutes' cooking time)

2,200 kJ/520 calories per portion

1 Put the rice into a sieve, rinse under cold running water, then drain. Wash the currants in hot water. Peel and finely chop the onion. Wash the liver in cold water, dry and cut into 1 cm dice.

2 In a large saucepan, heat 30 g of the butter. Add the onion and pine nuts and stir-fry over medium heat for about 3 minutes. Drain the currants and stir them into the pan with the rice, chicken stock, allspice and a little pepper, cinnamon and cumin. Cover and cook over low heat for about 10 minutes.

3 Meanwhile, heat the remaining 20 g butter in a frying pan, add the liver and toss over high heat for about 3 minutes, then stir it into the rice.

4 Continue to cook the rice, covered, for a further 10 minutes, then turn off the heat. Place a double layer of paper towel between the lid and the pan to absorb the steam, and leave the rice to stand on the hob for about 10 minutes.

5 Wash the dill and shake it dry. Finely chop the leaves and stir them into the rice. Season to taste with salt, and then serve at once.

Note: This dish, which has its origins in palace cuisine, is excellent on its own, or as an accompaniment to grilled lamb chops. It can also be made with chicken livers. Brown the livers in a frying pan and add to the rice about 5 minutes before the end of the cooking time.

Burghul pilaff

Easy · Central Anatolia   Bulgur pilavı

250 g coarsely ground burghul (cracked wheat)
2 small onions
3 long, pointed sweet peppers (see Glossary)
3 medium-sized tomatoes
40 g butter
1 tbsp tomato purée
1 tsp mild paprika
salt
freshly ground black pepper

Preparation time: 30 minutes
(plus 30 to 40 minutes' cooking time)

1,300 kJ/310 calories per portion

1 Pour the burghul into a sieve, rinse it under cold running water, and drain. Peel and finely chop the onions. Wash the peppers and then cut them in half lengthwise. Remove the stalk, seeds and ribs, then rinse the peppers and cut the flesh into shreds. Plunge the tomatoes into boiling water, leave them to stand briefly, then remove the skins and dice the flesh.

2 Heat the butter in a saucepan and sauté the onions until transparent, then add the shredded peppers and stir-fry over medium heat for about 2 minutes.

3 Add the tomatoes and cook briefly. Stir in the burghul, ¾ litre water, the tomato purée, paprika and salt to taste. Cook, uncovered, for about 10 minutes, stirring constantly.

4 Reduce the heat, cover the pan and continue to cook over low heat for a further 20 to 30 minutes. Turn off the heat, but leave the pan to stand on the hob for about 10 minutes.

5 Stir the burghul gently with a fork to separate the grains and then season to taste with salt and pepper.

Note: This pilaff is a good side dish to serve with grilled meatballs or kebabs. As a main course, cook diced lamb or veal with the burghul.

Mother-in-law's köfte

İçli köfte

2 small onions
50 g shelled walnuts • 30 g butter
225 g very finely minced lamb
15 g flat-leaf parsley
¼ tsp ground cinnamon
¼ tsp ground allspice
¼ tsp ground cumin
¼ tsp mild paprika
salt • freshly ground black pepper
sugar
150 g very finely ground burghul
(cracked wheat)
½ tsp ground coriander
½ litre sunflower oil for deep-frying

Preparation time: 1½ hours

2,600 kJ/620 calories per portion

1 Peel and very finely chop the onions. Coarsely chop the walnuts. Heat the butter in a frying pan and fry the onions over medium heat, until transparent. Stir in 100 g of the minced meat, break it up into very small pieces and stir-fry over high heat for 4 to 5 minutes, until browned. Remove from the heat. Wash the parsley, shake it dry and finely chop the leaves. Stir them into the meat with the walnuts and spices. Season to taste with salt, pepper and sugar.

2 Place the burghul in a bowl. Add the coriander and 14 cl warm water, then knead for at least 15 minutes. Sprinkle with salt and then knead to a dough with the remaining raw meat. Mince the dough, using the finest blade of the mincer, then knead again.

3 Divide the dough into 12 pieces and form the pieces into egg shapes with your hands. Hold each one in the palm of one hand and with the other index finger hollow it out to form a shell, like an empty eggshell, and stuff it with the cooked filling. Seal the hole by pinching the top with a twisting movement.

4 Heat the oil in a high-sided pan until small bubbles rise when a wooden chopstick is dipped in the oil. Deep-fry the *köfte* in batches of three until browned, then drain on paper towels. Serve hot or cold.

Burghul

Wheat has been grown in Anatolia since antiquity, when it was either cooked whole, or ground to make flour. Before the whole wheat could be eaten, however, it first had to be soaked for hours, then cooked for a long time. At some stage, canny cooks devised a labour-saving way of preparing wheat by making burghul, which, being partly processed, quickly rehydrates when soaked in water and becomes tender.

After each harvest, enough husked wheat was stored to last until the following year. It was first soaked in water, boiled then dried. Afterwards, the grains were finely or coarsely ground and packed in well-ventilated

cloth sacks, where they would keep for months. The wheat, when required, took only 30 minutes to prepare. While today's Turkish citydwellers generally buy ready-to-cook burghul, people in the villages still produce their own—a chore that usually involves the whole

family, armed with wooden pestles.

Coarsely ground burghul—also known as pourgouri, bulgur or cracked wheat—is cooked like rice. The finely ground variety is used in soups, salads and the popular soup base *tarhana (see page 34).*

Cheese-filled börek

More complex • Central Anatolia   Su böreği   *Serves 6*

For the dough:
500 g plain flour
4 eggs
2 tbsp lemon juice
1 tsp salt

For the filling:
200 g beyaz peynir (ewe's milk
cheese • see page 71)
30 g dill
30 g flat-leaf parsley
150 g butter for brushing,
plus extra for greasing the baking
dish
2 tbsp olive oil
14 cl milk

Preparation time: 2 hours
(plus 30 minutes' standing time
and 35 minutes' cooking time)

2,800 kJ/670 calories per portion

1 Sift the flour into a mixing bowl and make a well in the middle. Place the eggs, lemon juice, salt, and 5 cl water in the well. Working outwards from the middle, stir the ingredients together, then knead for about 5 minutes to make an elastic dough. Divide the dough into 12 pieces and shape them into balls. Arrange them on a floured board, cover with a damp cloth and leave to stand for at least 30 minutes.

2 Mash the cheese finely with a fork. Wash the dill and the parsley and shake them dry. Finely chop the leaves and stir them into the cheese.

3 Grease a 30 to 32 cm round—or rectangular, if preferred—baking dish. On a floured work surface, roll out one ball of dough into a paper-thin sheet slightly larger than the baking dish *(above)*, and use it to line the dish.

4 Roll out the rest of the dough balls to sheets the same size as the dish. Fill a

bowl with cold water. Preheat the oven to 220°(425°F or Mark 7). In a large saucepan, bring a generous quantity of water to the boil with the olive oil. Reserve one sheet of dough, then boil the remaining 10 sheets, one at a time, for about 2 minutes. When the dough rises to the surface of the water, remove it with a slotted spoon *(below, left)*, dip in cold water, then drain it on a tea towel.

5 Heat the butter and milk with a little salt, then brush the sheet of dough in the baking dish with the butter mixture.

6 Lay five sheets of cooked pastry one on top of the other in the dish, brushing each one with the butter mixture, then spread the cheese mixture over the top *(above).* Lay the remaining five cooked sheets over the filling, brushing each one with the butter mixture.

7 Fold the pastry overhanging the edge of the dish in towards the middle, brushing the edges with the butter and milk mixture. Place the uncooked sheet of dough on top. Brush the remaining butter mixture over the top.

8 Cut the pie into 8 cm squares, or similar-size shapes, and bake in the centre of the oven for 30 to 35 minutes, until golden-brown. Serve hot or cold.

Turkish-style pizzas

Lahmacun

Takes time • Southeastern Anatolia

Makes 8 (Serves 4)

450 g plain flour • salt
21 g fresh yeast
4 spring onions
2 large tomatoes (300 g)
2 mild or hot green chili peppers
(see Glossary)
60 g flat-leaf parsley
250 g very finely minced lamb
2 tsp pulbiber (flaked peppers)
¼ tsp ground cumin
freshly ground black pepper
2 tbsp olive oil
2 medium-sized red onions
1 tsp sumak (see Glossary)

*Preparation time: 1 hour
(plus 45 minutes' proving time and
40 to 60 minutes' cooking time)*

1,700 kJ/400 calories per portion

1 Sift the flour and a little salt into a bowl. In a separate bowl, dissolve the yeast in ¼ litre lukewarm water. Make a well in the middle of the flour, pour in the dissolved yeast and mix to a dough. Cover and leave to rise in a warm place for about 15 minutes. Then knead the dough for about 10 minutes, using your hands. Shape it into eight balls, cover and leave to prove in a warm place for about 30 minutes. Meanwhile, preheat the oven to 250°C (450°F or Mark 8).

2 Trim the spring onions, wash and finely chop them. Plunge the tomatoes into boiling water, leave them to stand briefly, then remove the skins and dice the flesh. Wash the chili peppers, cut in half lengthwise, removing the seeds and stalks, then rinse the chili peppers and cut into shreds. Wash the parsley and shake it dry. Divide it in half and finely chop the leaves of one half.

3 Knead the chopped vegetables and parsley with the minced meat, *pulbiber*, cumin and salt and pepper. Grease a large baking sheet. Divide the dough into eight pieces and roll out each one to a circle. Spread each circle with one eighth of the meat mixture and sprinkle with a little olive oil. Bake the pizzas two at a time on the baking sheet in the centre of the oven for 10 to 15 minutes.

4 Peel the red onions, cut them into thin rings and mix with the *sumak*. Tear the leaves from the rest of the parsley. Sprinkle the onion rings and parsley over the pizzas and serve at once.

Flat bread

Pide

Simple • Traditional

Makes 4

900 g plain flour
2 tsp salt
84 g fresh yeast
sunflower oil for greasing
4 tbsp semolina
1 egg
1 tsp sugar
1 tbsp olive oil
4 tbsp sesame seeds
1 tbsp çörekotu (nigella seeds)

*Preparation time: 45 minutes
(plus 40 minutes' proving time
and 20 to 25 minutes' cooking time)*

3,900 kJ/930 calories per loaf

1 Sift the flour and salt into a large mixing bowl. Dissolve the yeast in 60 cl lukewarm water, then stir it into the flour. Work to a smooth dough, then knead vigorously for about 5 minutes, until it no longer sticks to your fingers. Cover and leave to rise in a warm place for about 30 minutes.

2 Preheat the oven to 250°C (450°F or Mark 8). Grease two large baking sheets with sunflower oil. With floured hands, briefly knead the dough, then shape it into four balls. Spread a little flour and the semolina over the work surface. Using your hands, press each ball to make a flat loaf about 25 cm in diameter. Place two on each baking sheet. Cover the loaves and leave to prove for a further 10 minutes.

3 Whisk the egg with the sugar and olive oil. Oil the fingertips of one hand, press a diamond pattern in the loaves at 4 to 5 cm intervals, then brush with the egg mixture. Sprinkle the loaves with the sesame and nigella seeds. Bake them two at a time in the centre of the oven for 5 to 6 minutes, then open the oven door and quickly sprinkle ¼ cup water over the bottom of the oven. Close the door immediately and continue baking for 5 to 6 minutes, until the loaves are golden-brown.

Cigarette böreks

Quick • Istanbul   Sigara böreği   *Serves 4*

200 g beyaz peynir (ewe's milk cheese • see page 71)
30 g dill
30 g flat-leaf parsley
2 large sheets yufka pastry (see opposite page)
37.5 cl sunflower oil for frying

Preparation time: 40 minutes

2,500 kJ/600 calories per portion

1 Mash the cheese finely with a fork. Wash the dill and parsley and shake them dry. Finely chop the leaves and stir them into the cheese.

2 Spread the sheets of *yufka* pastry on a work surface. Lay one sheet on top of the other, then cut into quarters with a sharp knife. Cut each quarter into four equal triangles, as if slicing a cake.

3 Fill a saucer with cold water. Place 2 tsp of cheese filling at the long end of each triangle and fold the two corners inwards, then roll the pastry towards the point of the triangle, as if rolling a cigarette. Brush the point with a little cold water and press it down firmly to secure it to the roll.

4 Pour oil to a depth of 4 cm into a frying pan and heat it. Add the rolls and fry over high heat for about 5 minutes, until they are golden-brown all over. Drain on paper towels and serve hot.

Note: These cigarette-shaped fried pastries are very popular Turkish appetizers. They are also served with afternoon tea.

Yufka

Yufka is a thicker version of the crisp, golden, paper-thin pastry known as phyllo, used to make a variety of Middle Eastern and Greek sweet and savoury specialities. One of the best, and most widely, known of these sweets is *baklava*, a rich, multi-layered confection of buttered pastry, nuts and syrup.

In Turkey, *yufka* is produced by professional pastry makers known as *yufkacı*, but many Turkish cooks make their own at home. Rolling the dough is an art in itself, demanding many years of practice: the cook sits cross-legged on the floor in front of a large, round, wooden board, and rolls out the pastry with a long, thin rolling pin just 1.5 cm in diameter. In

the picture above, the women are also making *saç ekmeği*, a type of bread—similar to *yufka* but thicker and coarser in texture—whose recipe dates back to nomadic times. It is cooked above a wood fire in a *saç*, a round, domed baking sheet.

Phyllo is available fresh or frozen in supermarkets or specialist Greek and

Middle Eastern shops. Frozen phyllo—which should be thawed, still wrapped, in the refrigerator—dries out easily and becomes very brittle. Always keep any sheets that are waiting to be used covered with a damp cloth. Thawed phyllo will keep for about a week in the refrigerator; do not refreeze it.

Turkish ravioli

Mantı

Takes time • Central Anatolia

Serves 4

For the dough:
400 g plain flour
1 tsp salt
1 egg

For the filling:
*250 g very finely minced lamb
or beef*
1 medium-sized onion
30 g flat-leaf parsley
1 tsp mild paprika
ground cumin
salt
freshly ground black pepper

For the sauces:
525 g whole milk plain yogurt
100 g butter
1 tsp hot paprika
3 garlic cloves

**Preparation time: 2 hours
(plus 30 minutes' standing time)**

3,300 kJ/790 calories per portion

1 To make the dough, sift the flour into a mixing bowl. Stir in the salt, egg and 12.5 cl water and knead for 5 minutes to work the mixture to a smooth dough. Wrap in clingfilm and leave to stand for about 30 minutes.

2 To make the filling, place the meat in a bowl. Peel and finely chop the onion. Wash the parsley, shake it dry and then finely chop the leaves. Add the chopped onion and parsley to the meat. Season with the mild paprika, and cumin, salt and pepper to taste. Mix thoroughly.

3 Divide the dough into five pieces. On a floured work surface, roll out each piece until about 2 mm thick *(above)*.

4 Cut the dough into 4 cm squares. Place ½ tsp of the meat mixture on each square. Fold the four corners of the dough over the filling, pressing top and sides together between the thumb and index finger to form a bag *(above)*. Repeat until all the dough is used up.

5 Line a conical strainer with a coffee filter bag and suspend it over a bowl. Pour in the yogurt and leave it to drain for about 20 minutes.

6 Meanwhile, bring plenty of water to the boil in a large saucepan and cook the ravioli in batches, uncovered, over low heat for 4 to 5 minutes, until they float to the surface. Remove the cooked ravioli from the saucepan with a slotted spoon and leave them to drain briefly in a colander.

7 Heat the butter in a small frying pan and stir in the hot paprika. Pour the strained yogurt into a bowl. Peel and crush the garlic, and stir it into the yogurt. Add a little salt and stir well. Serve the ravioli on warm soup plates. Top each portion with the garlic yogurt and the hot paprika butter.

Drink: Chilled *ayran*, yogurt whisked with water, is the traditional drink to serve with Turkish ravioli.

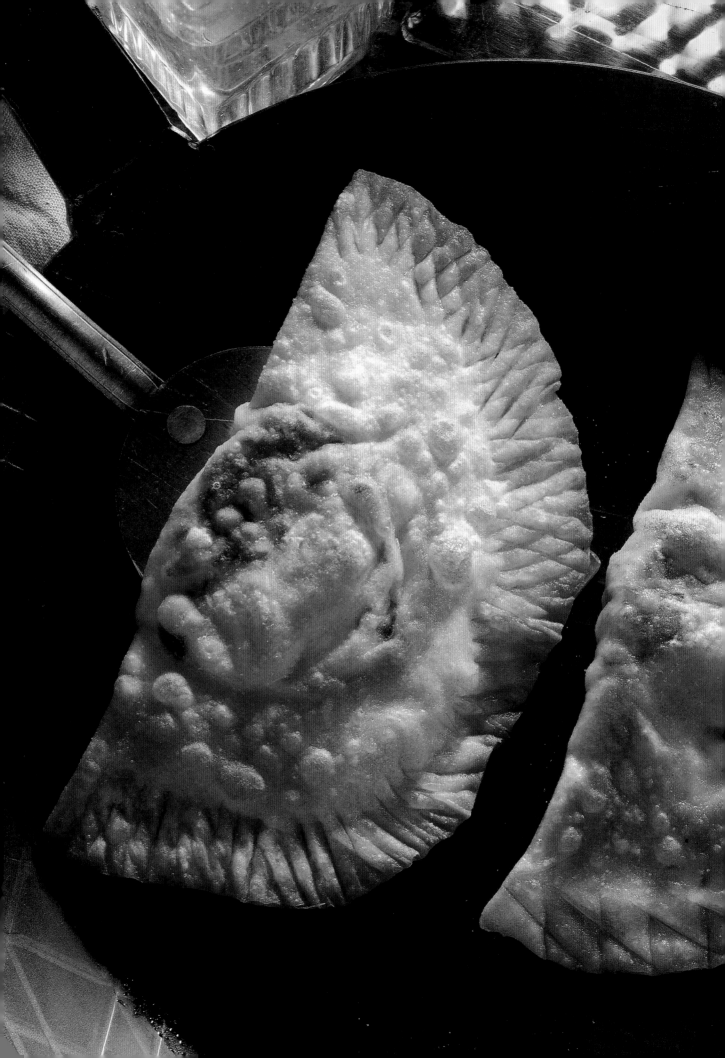

Pan-fried cheese pasties

Gözleme

Complicated • Mediterranean coast

Serves 4

150 g plain flour
1 ½ tsp salt
300 g leaf spinach
*150 g beyaz peynir or tulum peyniri
(see below)*
30 g flat-leaf parsley
10 cl sunflower oil for frying

*Preparation time: 1 hour
(plus 30 minutes' standing time)*

1,100 kJ/260 calories per portion

1 Sift the flour and salt into a bowl, then blend quickly with 10 cl warm water. Knead to a soft, smooth dough and shape it into 12 small balls. Place them on a floured board, cover with a damp cloth and leave to stand for about 30 minutes.

2 Meanwhile, sort the spinach, trim, wash and drain the leaves and cut them into thin strips. Place the cheese in a shallow bowl and mash finely with a fork. Wash the parsley and shake it dry. Finely chop the leaves and stir them into the cheese.

3 On a floured work surface, roll out the balls of dough to thin circles about 20 to 22 cm in diameter and carefully shake off any excess flour. On to one half of each circle, spoon 1 tbsp cheese and a little pile of spinach. Fold the other half of the dough over the filling and press the edges down firmly with a fork to seal and secure them.

4 Heat 1 to 2 tbsp oil in a frying pan and fry the pasties, in batches, over medium heat for about 5 minutes, until golden-brown on both sides.

Note: For extra flavour, brush the cooked pasties with melted butter.

Cheese

Most of Turkey's traditional cheeses are made from ewe's milk. The most popular is the creamy, salty, *beyaz peynir*. Pressed into blocks and preserved in brine, it has a fat content of between 35 and 75 per cent. This cheese is produced mainly in eastern Thrace, Eskişehir in central Anatolia, and Kars in eastern Anatolia. From this area, too, comes *kaşar peynir*, a cheese whose flavour strengthens as it matures. Made in large blocks, it is particularly good for slicing.

Tulum peyniri is a true nomad's cheese, mainly produced in the high *yayla* (summer pastures); wrapped in goatskin, it is hung up to dry so that it is pressed by its own weight.

A crumbly, salty cheese, it can be eaten on its own with bread, or used as a delicious filling for flaky pastry *(börek)* or pan-fried pasties *(gözleme)*.

More of a rarity is *dil peyniri*, a stringy, tongue-shaped cheese that is sometimes woven into skeins. It melts well and, being unsalted, is often used as a dessert ingredient. *Lor peyniri* is a goat's milk cheese; and *otlu peynir* (an eastern Anatolian speciality, produced in the region of Van) is a crumbly cream cheese, seasoned with wild garlic.

In Britain, feta cheese is the best substitute for these Turkish cheeses.

VEGETABLE DISHES

The coastal regions along the Aegean, the Sea of Marmara and the Mediterranean furnish the Turks with a wealth of vegetables, which consequently play a leading role in their cuisine. They are prepared in endlessly inventive ways, the types of dishes on offer varying according to the season. Only in the busier tourist areas are vegetables served merely as a decorative side dish, as a concession to European tastes.

Among the most popular specialities are vegetables cooked in olive oil and eaten cold. This type of dish is recognizable by words *zeytinyağlı* or *pilaki* in the recipe title. An exception to the rule is the intriguingly titled aubergine dish *imam bayıldı*, which translates as "the *imam* fainted". Legend has it that an *imam*, a prayer leader in the mosque, was so delighted by the aroma of this delicious creation that he fell into a swoon before it.

Turkish vegetable dishes owe their characteristic flavour to carefully balanced seasoning, which requires the use of almost equal quantities of salt and sugar. They may be served as a starter, an in-between course, or as a light summer main course. In the winter, white or borlotti beans, carrots, celery and leeks are all prepared in a similar way.

Okra in olive oil

Zeytinyağlı bamya   *Serves 4*

750 g very small okra
4 tbsp wine vinegar
salt
1 medium-sized onion
1 long, pointed sweet pepper (see Glossary)
1 tsp sugar
juice of 1 lemon
6 tbsp virgin olive oil
2 large tomatoes
30 g flat-leaf parsley for garnish

Preparation time: 40 minutes (plus 20 minutes' soaking time, 30 minutes' cooking time, and cooling time)

890 kJ/210 calories per portion

1 Wash the okra thoroughly and pat dry then, using a sharp kitchen knife, carefully peel the okra stalks to a point *(above)*, as if sharpening a pencil. Take care not to split the okra, otherwise the dish will be slimy. Place the peeled okra in a bowl. Stir in the vinegar and a generous 1 tsp salt, and leave to soak for about 20 minutes.

2 Meanwhile, peel the onion. Remove the stalk and seeds from the pepper, then rinse it. Rinse the okra thoroughly and drain them. Arrange them in a circular pattern in a wide pan, with the sharp ends pointing inwards, leaving a space in the middle. Place the whole onion and whole pepper in the central space between the okra *(above)*, and sprinkle the sugar and a scant 1 tsp salt over the top of the vegetables. Pour the lemon juice, olive oil and 5 cl water over the okra.

3 Cover the vegetables with a piece of greaseproof paper, then place the lid on the pan and cook the okra over low heat for about 30 minutes, giving the pan a gentle shake from time to time. Leave the vegetables to cool in the pan.

4 Before serving, wash the tomatoes. Cut them into eighths, removing the hard flesh under the stalk. Wash the parsley, shake it dry and tear off the leaves. Arrange the vegetables on a serving dish and garnish with a ring of tomatoes and parsley leaves. Serve with *pide* (flat bread, *see page 65*).

Wine: A well-chilled, medium dry rosé, such as Kavaklıdere Rosato, goes well with this vegetable dish.

Note: In order to be able to enjoy this very popular vegetable throughout the winter, the Turks dry okra by threading them by their stalks onto a string, like pearls on a necklace. Only the very smallest okra, about 1.5 cm long, are dried. In the *bakkal*, or grocer's shop, chains of okra can be seen dangling from the ceiling or attached to shelves. Dried okra is soaked overnight in plenty of water before cooking. It is good cooked with tomatoes and meat, and served hot.

Artichokes in olive oil

Takes time • Istanbul   **Zeytinyağlı enginar**   *Serves 4*

2 lemons
1 tbsp flour
4 large round artichokes (about 1 kg)
4 shallots
1 large carrot
100 g celeriac
6 tbsp virgin olive oil
1 scant tsp salt
1 tsp sugar
freshly ground black pepper
30 g dill
50 g frozen peas

Preparation time: 40 minutes (plus 40 minutes' cooking time, and cooling time)

1,300 kJ/310 calories per portion

1 Squeeze one of the lemons and pour the juice into a wide saucepan. Add ½ litre cold water and whisk in the flour, using a hand whisk. Wash the artichokes thoroughly. Cut off the leaves, so that only those about 5 mm from the base remain, and then scoop out the chokes with a spoon. Cut the second lemon in half. Rinse the inside of the artichokes and rub with the lemon, to stop them turning brown.

2 Trim the artichoke stalks, leaving stumps about 2 cm long, and peel them thinly. Place the artichokes in the pan of water. Peel and finely chop the shallots. Wash, trim and peel the carrot and celeriac, and chop them into small dice. Sprinkle the chopped vegetables over the artichokes.

3 Mix the olive oil with the salt and the sugar. Drizzle it over the vegetables and sprinkle with pepper. Cover and cook over medium heat for 30 minutes.

4 Meanwhile, wash the dill, shake it dry and tear off the leaves. Rinse the peas in a colander. Add half the dill and the drained peas to the vegetables in the pan. Continue to cook for a further 10 minutes, then leave the vegetables to cool in the pan.

5 Arrange one artichoke on each plate, with the stalk upwards. Sprinkle with the rest of the vegetables and a little stock. Garnish with the rest of the dill. Serve as a starter or vegetable course.

Wine: A dry white wine, such as a Kavaklidere Muscat from the Aegean region, is a good choice with this dish.

Leeks in olive oil

Not difficult • Aegean coast **Zeytinyağlı pirasa** *Serves 4 to 6*

1 kg leeks, preferably thin ones
2 medium-sized carrots
6 tbsp olive oil
4 tbsp long-grain rice
1 scant tsp salt
1 tsp sugar
1 lemon

Preparation time: 20 minutes
(plus 40 minutes' cooking time, and
cooling time)

710 kJ/170 calories per portion
(if serving 6)

1 Trim the leeks, removing the green leaves and the outer layer of the white parts. Wash the leeks while still whole, preferably without cutting them open, then cut into pieces about 5 cm long. Trim, peel and finely chop the carrots.

2 Heat the oil in a saucepan and stir-fry the vegetables over medium heat for about 10 minutes. Add ½ litre water and bring it to the boil. Rinse the rice in a sieve. Stir the rice, salt and sugar into the vegetables. Cover the saucepan and cook the rice and vegetables over low heat for about 30 minutes, stirring carefully from time to time.

3 Transfer the vegetables to a bowl and leave them to cool. This dish can be eaten warm or cold. Before serving, wash the lemon in hot water and cut it into eight wedges. At the table, sprinkle a few drops of lemon juice over each portion of leeks.

Drink: Chilled *ayran*, yogurt whisked with water, is good with this dish.

Variation: A large, waxy potato, cut into dice, can be cooked with the leeks.

Borlotti beans in olive oil

Barbunya pilakisi

Takes time • Hearty

Serves 4 to 6

1 kg fresh or 250 g dried borlotti beans
1 medium-sized onion
8 garlic cloves
2 medium-sized carrots
1 medium-sized potato
6 tbsp olive oil
1 tbsp tomato purée • 1 tsp sugar
salt • freshly ground black pepper
15 g flat-leaf parsley • 1 lemon

Preparation time: 40 minutes (plus 12 hours for soaking the beans, 45 minutes' cooking time, and cooling time)

2,000 kJ/480 calories per portion (if serving 6)

1 If you are using fresh beans, shell them and rinse them in a colander. If using dried beans, soak them overnight in plenty of cold water, then rinse well. Whether using fresh or dried beans, place them in a saucepan with enough water to cover and precook them over low heat for about 30 minutes.

2 Meanwhile, peel the onion and garlic. Wash and peel the carrots and potato. Finely chop the onion. Chop the carrots and potato into 1 cm dice. Heat the olive oil in a second saucepan and fry the onion over medium heat until transparent. Stir in the whole garlic cloves and the rest of the vegetables, and cook for about 2 minutes. Add the tomato purée, sugar and a generous amount of salt and pepper, and stir thoroughly. Add ¾ litre water and bring to the boil. Drain the beans while still hot and stir them into the vegetables. Cover and simmer for 30 to 40 minutes, until the vegetables are tender, taking care not to let the beans fall apart.

3 Transfer the contents of the pan to a serving dish. Cover and leave until cold. Wash the parsley, shake it dry, and tear off the leaves. Cut the lemon into eight wedges. Garnish the dish with parsley and serve with lemon wedges.

Note: Dried white beans can be cooked and served in the same way.

Green beans with tomato

Zeytinyağlı taze fasulye

Not difficult • Coastal regions

Serves 4

750 g flat green beans
2 medium-sized onions
2 large tomatoes
1 tbsp tomato purée
6 tbsp olive oil
1 tsp sugar
1 scant tsp salt
1 unwaxed lemon

Preparation time: 45 minutes (plus 25 to 35 minutes' cooking time, and cooling time)

1,000 kJ/240 calories per portion

1 Wash, trim and string the beans. Cut them into pieces 4 to 5 cm long. Peel and finely chop the onions. Plunge the tomatoes into boiling water, leave them to stand briefly, then remove the skins. Cut the tomatoes in half and dice the flesh. Reserve the juice.

2 Place the prepared beans, onions and tomatoes in a saucepan and stir in the tomato purée and juice, olive oil, sugar and salt. Mix well. Cover the pan and cook over high heat for 5 minutes, shaking the pan from time to time, to prevent the vegetables sticking.

3 Add ¼ litre water to the beans. Stir, then continue to cook, covered, over medium heat for 20 to 30 minutes, until the beans are tender. Transfer them to a bowl. Wash the lemon in hot water, slice thinly, then arrange the slices on top of the beans and leave the mixture to cool completely.

4 When the beans are cool, squeeze the juice from the lemon slices over them, then discard the lemon slices. Serve the beans with crusty white bread. Ewe's milk cheese is also a good accompaniment to serve with this cold vegetable dish.

Note: When trimming the beans, cut a thin strip all the way round the edges to remove the strings completely.

Stuffed vine leaves
Zeytinyağlı yaprak dolması

Serves 4 to 6

250 g fresh or preserved vine leaves
salt
120 g long-grain rice
1 tbsp very small currants (kuş üzümü)
1 medium-sized onion
8 tbsp virgin olive oil
30 g pine-nuts
½ tsp ground cinnamon
¼ tsp ground allspice
½ tsp sugar
30 g flat-leaf parsley
30 g dill
½ unwaxed lemon

Preparation time: 1 hour
(plus 45 minutes' cooking time)

1,000 kJ/240 calories per portion
(if serving 6)

1 Separate the vine leaves and arrange them loosely in a saucepan of salted boiling water. Boil fresh vine leaves for about 1 minute. If you are using preserved vine leaves, simmer them for about 5 minutes. In either case, leave the leaves to stand in a bowl of cold water when cooked.

2 Rinse and drain the rice in a sieve. Wash the currants in hot water. Peel and finely grate the onion. Heat 4 tbsp olive oil in a saucepan and sauté the grated onion over medium heat until transparent. Stir in the rice and cook for about 1 minute.

3 Add the pine-nuts and stir-fry until they turn yellow. Stir in the drained currants, cinnamon, allspice, sugar and ½ tsp salt. Add 35 cl water and bring to the boil. Cover and cook over low heat for about 15 minutes, until all the water is absorbed. Remove the lid and leave the rice to cool in the pan.

4 Wash the parsley and dill, shake dry, then finely chop half the herb leaves. Stir them into the rice.

5 Remove the vine leaves from the bowl of water and spread them out on paper towels. Cut off the stalks. Line the bottom of a medium-sized saucepan or fireproof casserole with three or four vine leaves. (You can use the less attractive leaves for this.)

6 Place 1 generous tsp of rice at the stalk end of each vine leaf on the paper towels. Fold over the left and right edges to cover the filling, then roll up the vine leaf towards the tip *(above)*.

7 Place the rolled-up vine leaves close together in the pan or casserole, with the leaf points downwards. Once the bottom of the pan is full, arrange the rest of the rolls in layers on top *(above)*. Sprinkle with 4 tbsp olive oil. Wash the half lemon in hot water and then slice it thinly. Arrange the lemon slices on top of the vine leaves.

8 Add ¼ litre water to the pan and place an upturned plate on the vine leaves to weigh them down. Cover the pan and cook over low heat for about 30 minutes. Leave the vine leaves to cool in the pan, then remove the lemon slices. Transfer the vine leaves to a serving dish and garnish with the rest of the parsley and dill.

Broad beans in olive oil

Zeytinyağlı taze bakla

**700 g fresh, very young broad
beans in their pods**
1 medium-sized onion
6 tbsp olive oil
1 tsp flour
½ tsp sugar
½ tsp salt
30 g dill
juice of ½ lemon
350 g whole milk plain yogurt

**Preparation time: 45 minutes
(plus 30 minutes' cooking time, and
cooling time)**

**2,300 kJ/550 calories
per portion**

1 Wash the broad beans thoroughly, then trim and string them. Peel and finely grate the onion. Heat the olive oil in a saucepan and sauté the onion until transparent. Add the broad beans.

2 Mix the flour with ¼ litre water and stir until it is smooth. Pour the flour mixture over the beans and bring to the boil, stirring constantly.

3 Stir in the sugar and salt, and cook the beans over low heat for 25 minutes, or until tender (the cooking time will depend on the thickness of the pods).

4 Wash the dill, then shake it dry and coarsely chop all but one sprig. About 5 minutes before the end of the cooking time, stir the lemon juice and chopped dill into the beans. Transfer the beans to a serving dish and leave to cool.

5 Tear the leaves from the remaining sprig of dill and sprinkle them over the beans. Pour the yogurt into a bowl and whisk with a hand whisk until creamy. Serve the yogurt with the cold beans. At the table, each person adds 2 to 3 tbsp of yogurt to the beans and eats them together. Alternatively, pour the yogurt over the beans in the serving dish and sprinkle with the dill leaves.

Winter vegetable hotpot

Takes time • Hearty ## Kış türlüsü

Serves 4

2 large potatoes
2 large carrots
2 sweet potatoes (about 300 g)
250 g celeriac
2 medium-sized onions
2 thin leeks
8 tbsp olive oil
120 g long-grain rice
1 scant tsp salt
1 scant tsp sugar
½ tsp mild paprika
freshly ground black pepper
15 g flat-leaf parsley
15 g dill

**Preparation time: 45 minutes
(plus 40 minutes´ cooking time
and cooling time)**

**1,900 kJ/450 calories
per portion**

1 Trim, wash and peel the potatoes, carrots, sweet potatoes and celeriac, and cut them into 2 to 3 cm cubes. Peel and finely chop the onions. Trim the leeks, removing the tough, outer green leaves. Wash the leeks thoroughly and cut them into pieces about 2 cm long.

2 Heat the olive oil in a saucepan and sauté the vegetables over medium heat for about 10 minutes, stirring from time to time. Pour the rice into a sieve and rinse it under cold running water, then add it to the vegetables. Add ¼ litre water. Season with the salt, sugar and paprika, and plenty of pepper.

3 Cook the vegetables over low heat for about 30 minutes, stirring them occasionally. Do not allow them to fall

apart. If necessary, add another 12.5 cl to ¼ litre hot water during the cooking time to keep the vegetables moist.

4 Leave the vegetables to cool in the pan, or transfer them to a serving bowl. Wash the parsley and dill, shake them dry and finely chop the leaves. Sprinkle the chopped leaves over the vegetables before serving.

Drink: Chilled *ayran*, yogurt whisked with water, or beer, goes well with this very nourishing winter hotpot.

Note: This dish is served as a main course. It is usually eaten warm or cold, but is equally delicious piping hot.

Stuffed aubergines

Not difficult • Istanbul İmam bayıldı *Serves 4*

4 aubergines (about 800 g)
salt
2 medium-sized onions
2 large tomatoes
45 g flat-leaf parsley
4 mild green chili peppers (see Glossary)
4 garlic cloves
8 tbsp olive oil
½ tsp sugar

Preparation time: 45 minutes (plus 45 minutes' cooking time, and cooling time)

910 kJ/220 calories per portion

1 Wash the aubergines. Trim off the leaves around the stalks and thinly peel the stalks. Peel away the aubergine skin lengthwise in strips at intervals of about 2 to 3 cm, to create a striped effect *(above)*.

2 Make a long, deep incision in one of the peeled strips on each aubergine, to provide a pocket for the stuffing. Soak the aubergines in cold, salted water for 15 minutes.

3 Meanwhile, peel the onions and slice them. Plunge the tomatoes into boiling water, leave to stand briefly, then remove the skins and cut them in half. Dice the flesh and reserve the juice. Wash the parsley and shake it dry. Finely chop the leaves of two thirds of it. Tear off the leaves of the remainder and reserve them for the garnish.

4 Wash the chili peppers, cut them in half lengthwise, remove the stalks and seeds, then rinse them. Peel the garlic and cut the cloves into matchsticks. Dry the aubergines.

5 Heat 3 tbsp olive oil in a frying pan. Fry the aubergines over medium heat for 5 to 7 minutes, until lightly browned all over. Transfer them to a shallow fireproof casserole or pot and arrange them with the incision upwards.

6 Heat another 2 tbsp oil in the same frying pan and fry the sliced onions over medium heat until transparent. Remove from the heat and stir in the tomatoes with their reserved juice, the chopped parsley, ½ tsp salt, the sugar and the remaining 3 tbsp olive oil. Fill the pockets in the aubergines with some of the vegetable mixture *(below)*.

7 Spread the remaining vegetables over the top of the aubergines and sprinkle them with the pan juices. Spike the filling with the garlic.

8 Arrange two chili halves on top of each aubergine, and pour over ¼ litre water. Bring to the boil and cook over medium heat for 10 minutes, then simmer over low heat for 35 minutes. Leave to cool, transfer to a serving dish, and garnish with parsley leaves.

Wine: Choose a dry, fresh white wine, such as a Kavaklıdere Çankaya.

Note: There are several versions of how this dish acquired its name, which translates as "the *imam* [a Muslim religious leader] fainted". One says that this frugal holy man fainted with delight at the aroma, another that he ate so much of it that he passed out, and a third that he fainted with shock at the sheer cost of the olive oil used.

FISH AND SEAFOOD

T he Turks' great love of the
sea and of its myriad delights
is easily understood when you
consider the nomadic past of their
ancestors. Having wandered for so long
over the endless grassy steppes
of central Asia, these early tribes must
have been both astonished and
delighted when they came upon the
richly stocked seas that encircle the
peninsula of Asia Minor.

Today, fish and seafood are still
valued as a special gift, and seasonal
specialities are eagerly awaited. In
winter, mackerel, sea perch, *hamsi*
(a type of anchovy) and mussels are
enjoyed; and in summer, anchovies, sea
bass, rosefish and swordfish are on
offer. Each sea has its own local breeds
of fish, in addition to others common to
all; on the Bosphorus, anglers can be
seen patiently waiting for fish passing
from the Black Sea to the
Mediterranean—or vice versa.

Methods of preparation are many:
fish grilled over charcoal and served
with tomatoes, red onions and rocket
is particularly popular, and the Turkish
preference for food cooked in olive oil
and eaten cold also applies to fish and
shellfish. Oven baking is another
favourite: dishes that can be served
straight from the oven include prawn
gratin and enticing little parcels of fish
wrapped in greaseproof paper.

Sardines in vine leaves

Easy • Aegean coast   Asma yaprağında sardalya   *Serves 4*

800 g gutted, fresh, medium-sized sardines (about 24 fish)
salt
48 fresh or preserved vine leaves
6 tbsp virgin olive oil, plus extra for brushing
freshly ground black pepper
60 g flat-leaf parsley
juice of 2 lemons

Preparation time: 45 minutes

1,700 kJ/400 calories per portion

1 Scale the sardines, rinse them under cold running water and dry them inside and out. Sprinkle them inside and out with a little salt and leave to stand briefly. If using preserved vine leaves, soak them in cold water for about 10 minutes. If using fresh ones, rinse them under cold running water. Spread out the leaves on paper towels, smooth side upwards, and brush them with olive oil. Preheat the grill.

2 Wipe the sardines with paper towels, then sprinkle them inside and out with pepper. Wash the parsley and shake it dry. Separate the sprigs from half the parsley and lay sprigs inside each sardine. Wrap each sardine in two vine leaves and secure with a small wooden skewer. Brush with olive oil.

3 Arrange the sardines side by side on the grid of the grill pan. Grill them for 6 to 8 minutes on each side, depending on their size. Chop the remaining parsley and place it in a bowl. Stir the lemon juice, the rest of the olive oil and 3 to 4 tbsp water together with the chopped parsley to make a dressing.

4 Transfer the sardines to individual serving plates, then undo the vine leaf wrappings and sprinkle the sardines with the dressing. Serve with *pide* (flat bread, *see page 65*) or white bread.

Drink: Serve the sardines with *rakı*, or a dry white wine such as Villa Neva.

Swordfish kebabs

Kılıçbalığı şişte

Takes time • Coastal regions

Serves 4

800 g swordfish steaks
1 large onion
2 tbsp lemon juice
4 tbsp virgin olive oil
salt
freshly ground black pepper
3 mild green chili peppers (see Glossary)
1 unwaxed lemon
12 bay leaves

Preparation time: 45 minutes (plus 1 hour's marinating time)

1,100 kJ/260 calories per portion

1 Rinse the fish under cold running water, pat it dry with paper towels, then cut it into 2.5 cm cubes. Peel the onion and grate it into a bowl. Stir in the lemon juice and olive oil, and season to taste with salt and pepper. Turn the cubes of fish in the marinade, then leave them to marinate in a cool place for about 1 hour.

2 Remove the stalks and the hard part under the stalks from the chilis. Wash them and cut the flesh, with the seeds, into 2.5 cm lengths.

3 Wash the lemon in hot water and slice it—the slices should be thin enough to fold easily. Preheat the grill.

Brush four long metal skewers with a little of the marinade.

4 Thread the fish cubes, chili peppers, bay leaves and folded lemon slices alternately onto the skewers. Grill for 5 to 6 minutes on each side.

Drink: Serve with *rakı* or well-chilled, dry white wine such as a Moskado Sek.

Note: Garnish the grilled kebabs with tomato wedges or rocket. In Turkey, the delicately sour, slightly piquant-flavoured rocket is a very popular accompaniment to fish, and diners in local fish restaurants often order extra portions of it with their meal.

Sea bass parcels

Levrek kağıtta

800 g sea bass or rosefish fillet
80 g butter
salt
freshly ground black pepper
2 large tomatoes
30 g flat-leaf parsley
1 unwaxed lemon

Preparation time: 30 minutes
(plus 25 minutes' cooking time)

1,600 kJ/380 calories per portion

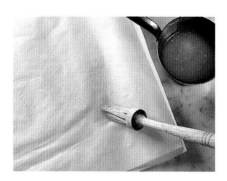

1 Preheat the oven to 175°C (350°F or Mark 4). Rinse the fish under cold running water, dry with paper towels, then cut into eight equal-sized pieces. Melt 40 g of the butter in a frying pan. Cut eight sheets of greaseproof paper large enough to wrap the fish in. Place the sheets in four lots of two. Brush the upper sides with butter *(above)*.

2 Lay one piece of fish on each double layer of paper and sprinkle lightly with salt and pepper. Wash the tomatoes. Slice each tomato into four pieces, removing the hard flesh under the stalk. Place two slices of tomato on each piece of fish, season lightly with salt and pepper, then top each one with a second piece of fish *(above)*.

3 Flake the rest of the butter over the fish. Wash the parsley and shake it dry. Arrange a few parsley leaves on top of each portion, then sprinkle with salt and pepper. Wash the lemon in hot water, cut 4 thin slices and place one on each portion of fish. Wrap the greaseproof paper over the fish.

4 Twist the ends of the paper to a point, and fold the point under the parcel *(above)*. Bake the fish parcels on a grid in the centre of the oven for 20 to 25 minutes, according to the thickness of the fillets. Lay the parcels on warmed plates and open them very carefully. Sprinkle the remaining parsley leaves over the fish and serve in the paper wrapping, accompanied by freshly baked white bread or *pide* (flat bread, *see page 65*).

Wine: A well-chilled, dry white wine, such as a light Villa Neva from the Marmara region, is good with this dish.

Grilled ocean perch

Easy • Istanbul   Lüfer ızgarası   *Serves 4*

4 ocean perch or mackerel, cleaned
2 medium-sized white onions
30 g flat-leaf parsley
salt
freshly ground black pepper
2 tsp sunflower oil for brushing
60 g rocket
2 medium-sized red onions
1 unwaxed lemon

**Preparation time: 30 minutes
(plus 30 minutes' standing time)**

2,100 kJ/500 calories per portion

1 Rinse the fish, inside and out, under cold running water and pat dry. Peel the white onions and slice them very thinly. Wash the parsley and shake it dry. Chop the leaves and add them to the onion. Sprinkle with salt and pepper, and mix together with your hands. Stuff the body cavity of each fish with the onion mixture. Sprinkle the outsides of the fish with salt, then leave to stand for about 30 minutes. Meanwhile, preheat the grill.

2 Pat the fish dry with paper towels. Make several incisions along the fleshy part of the back. Brush with the oil.

3 Wash the rocket, shake it dry and arrange on four oval individual plates. Peel and quarter the red onions. Wash

the lemon in hot water and cut it into eight wedges.

4 Place the fish on the grid in the grill pan and grill for 6 to 8 minutes on each side, according to size. (They are ready when the back fins can be pulled off easily.) Arrange the fish on the plates with the rocket. Add two pieces of onion and two lemon wedges to each plate, and serve immediately.

Drink: Natives of Istanbul drink *rakı* with this dish, but a dry white wine such as Villa Doluca is equally good.

Fish

The long Turkish coastline includes the Black Sea, the Aegean and the Mediterranean, affording the Turks an exceptionally rich variety of fresh fish *(balik)*. The Sea of Marmara and the Bosphorus, on which Istanbul stands, are also well stocked, giving the city's inhabitants a choice of fish from cool or warm waters. North of Istanbul, in the waterfront town of Sariyer, the fishermen know from experience exactly which shoals of fish to expect, and when. Favourites among the locals are *lüfer* (ocean perch) and *palamut* (bonito), either grilled or cooked with vegetables.

The Black Sea yields *levrek* (sea bass), *kalkan* (turbot) and *zargana* (garfish), which has vivid green bones even when cooked. A favourite speciality in the coastal resorts of this region is *hamsi*, a type of anchovy; in winter these little silvery fish appear in large numbers close to the coast and in the Bosphorus. From the Aegean and Mediterranean seas come *kılıçbalığı*, the very popular swordfish, *mercan* (red sea bream), *barbunya* (red mullet), *karagöz* (sargo), *kefal* (grey mullet) and many others.

Fresh fish is available inland, too, where trout are reared in the mountain streams. They are served either grilled, or fried in butter or olive oil. The central Anatolian lakes also provide northern Europe with regular supplies of crayfish.

Baked red mullet

Barbunya buğulaması

Takes time • Prepare in advance

Serves 4 to 6

1 kg red mullet, cleaned
salt
freshly ground black pepper
5 tbsp olive oil
4 medium-sized tomatoes
2 medium-sized onions
30 g flat-leaf parsley
1 unwaxed lemon
3 bay leaves

Preparation time: 20 minutes
(plus 35 to 45 minutes' cooking time)

1,200 kJ/290 calories per portion (if serving 6)

1 Preheat the oven to 200°C (400°F or Mark 6). Rinse the fish, inside and out, under cold running water, pat them dry on paper towels, then sprinkle with salt and pepper. Brush a large baking dish with 2 tbsp of the olive oil. Lay the fish side by side in the dish.

2 Wash and slice the tomatoes. Peel the onions and cut into thin rings.

3 Wash the parsley, shake dry and chop the leaves. Sprinkle them over the fish, then drizzle the remaining olive oil on top. Wash the lemon in hot water, then slice it. Place the lemon slices and bay leaves on top of the fish. Cover with an alternating pattern of sliced tomatoes and onions rings, and sprinkle with salt and pepper. Tightly cover the dish with greaseproof paper or aluminium foil.

4 Bake the red mullet in the centre of the oven for 30 to 40 minutes, then turn the oven up to 225°C (425°F or Mark 7). Remove the paper or foil and bake the fish, uncovered, for a further 5 minutes. Serve straight from the dish with *pide* (flat bread, *see page 65*).

Wine: A dry rosé wine, such as a Kavaklıdere Lal from the Aegean hinterland, is a good choice to serve with this dish.

Grey mullet with olive oil

Kefal pilakisi

Easy • Mediterranean coast

Serves 4

1 kg grey mullet, cleaned
2 medium-sized onions
3 garlic cloves
3 medium-sized carrots
3 potatoes (about 300 g)
6 tbsp olive oil
2 medium-sized tomatoes
1 tsp tomato purée
½ tsp sugar
salt • freshly ground black pepper
2 unwaxed lemons
15 g parsley
15 g dill

Preparation time: 30 minutes
(plus 30 minutes' cooking time)

1,800 kJ/430 calories per portion

1 Rinse the fish, inside and out, under cold running water and pat dry. Using kitchen scissors, cut off the fins and heads. Cut the grey mullet, including the bones, into 2 cm pieces.

2 Peel and thinly slice the onions and garlic. Peel the carrots and potatoes and cut them into 2 cm pieces. Heat the olive oil in a high-sided frying pan. Stir-fry the vegetables over medium heat for about 10 minutes.

3 Plunge the tomatoes into boiling water, leave to stand briefly, then skin them. Chop the flesh finely and add it to the vegetables in the pan. Stir in the tomato purée, sugar and 12.5 cl water. Season with salt and pepper. Lay the fish pieces among the vegetables.

4 Wash the lemons in hot water, then thinly slice one of them and cover the fish with the slices. Cover the frying pan and cook over low heat for about 30 minutes. Wash the parsley and dill, shake dry, and chop the leaves. Cut the remaining lemon into eight wedges. When the fish is cooked, remove the lemon slices and stir in the chopped herbs. Serve warm, garnished with the lemon wedges so that the fish can be sprinkled with lemon juice at the table.

Note: Hake or cod can be used instead of grey mullet, if preferred.

Mussels with walnut sauce

Taratorlu midye tavası

Takes time • Istanbul

Serves 4

100 g shelled walnuts
2 slices (80 g) white bread
juice of 1 lemon
2 tbsp sunflower oil
2 tbsp walnut oil
1 garlic clove
salt
1.5 kg fresh mussels
6 tbsp plain flour
1 tbsp cornflour
1 egg yolk
about 4 tbsp lager or light ale
1 cos lettuce
37.5 cl sunflower oil for deep-frying

Preparation time: 2 hours

2,500 kJ/600 calories per portion

1 To make the sauce, finely chop the walnuts in a food processor. Cut off the bread crusts. Soften the slices of bread in a little water, then squeeze out as much moisture as possible. Add the bread, lemon juice and the 2 tbsp of each oil to the walnuts. Peel and crush the garlic, and stir it into the mixture. Stir in enough water to create a thick sauce, then season with salt.

2 Scrape, wash and then beard the mussels. Tap any mussels that are open and discard any that do not close. Bring ¼ litre salted water to the boil in a large saucepan. Add the mussels, cover and cook them over high heat for 5 to 7 minutes, until the shells open, shaking the pan from time to time. Discard any that remain closed.

3 Leave the cooked mussels to cool, then shell them. Sift 3 tbsp of the flour on to a plate. Coat the mussels in the flour, shaking off any excess. Mix together the remaining flour, cornflour, egg yolk and enough lager to make a thin batter. Season it lightly with salt.

4 Cut out the heart of the cos lettuce, wash it and shake dry. Arrange the leaves in a dish with the walnut sauce.

5 Heat the 37.5 cl oil in a frying pan, until small bubbles rise from a wooden skewer dipped in the oil. Thread three or four mussels onto each of eight wooden skewers. Dip in the batter and then deep-fry for 2 to 4 minutes, until golden. Drain on paper towels, then serve with the walnut sauce.

Prawn gratin

Karides güveci

Easy • Istanbul

Serves 4

4 shallots
2 garlic cloves
2 large tomatoes
2 long, pointed sweet peppers (see Glossary)
60 g butter
2 bay leaves
12.5 cl dry white wine
salt • freshly ground black pepper
cayenne pepper
500 g cooked peeled prawns
4 tbsp freshly grated kaşar or emmenthal cheese

Preparation time: 45 minutes

1,300 kJ/310 calories per portion

1 Peel and finely chop the shallots and the garlic. Plunge the tomatoes into boiling water, leave to stand briefly, then skin them and chop the flesh. Wash the sweet peppers, cut them in half lengthwise and remove the stalks, seeds and ribs. Rinse them again and cut into thin strips.

2 Preheat the oven to 220°C (425°F or Mark 7) and grease four individual earthenware dishes with 30 g of the butter. Heat the rest of the butter in a frying pan. Tear the bay leaves in half and briefly brown them in the frying pan. Add all the vegetables and stir-fry over high heat for about 1 minute. Add

the wine, bring to the boil and continue cooking over low heat for 1 minute. Season to taste with salt and pepper and a little cayenne pepper.

3 Stir the prawns into the vegetables and briefly heat through. Divide the mixture between the dishes. Sprinkle the cheese over the top and bake in the centre of the oven for about 8 minutes, until the cheese begins to brown. Serve at once with fresh baguettes or *pide* (flat bread, *see page 65*).

Wine: A chilled rosé such as Doluca is an excellent choice to serve with this tasty prawn dish.

Stuffed mussels

Midye dolması

Serves 4

20 large, closed mussels
salt
50 g long-grain rice
1 tbsp very small currants (kuş üzümü)
3 shallots
4 tbsp olive oil
1 tbsp pine-nuts
½ tsp dried mint
cinnamon
allspice
sugar
2 sprigs dill
1 unwaxed lemon
30 g flat-leaf parsley

Preparation time: 40 minutes (plus 35 minutes' cooking time, and cooling time)

960 kJ/230 calories per portion)

1 Scrub the mussels under cold running water, removing the beards *(above)*. Discard any that are open. Bring ¼ litre salted water to the boil in a large saucepan. Add the mussels, cover the pan and cook over high heat for 5 to 7 minutes, until the mussels open, shaking the pan from time to time. Pour the mussels into a sieve and leave them to cool. Discard any mussels that are still closed.

2 Place the rice in a sieve, rinse under cold running water, then drain. Wash the currants in hot water. Peel and finely chop the shallots. Heat the olive oil in a large saucepan and sauté the shallots until transparent.

3 Add the pine-nuts and the rice, and fry for about 1 minute over medium heat. Stir in the currants and dried mint and a little cinnamon, allspice, sugar and salt. Add 12.5 cl water, cover the pan and cook over low heat for about 20 minutes.

4 Leave the rice to cool. Wash the dill and shake it dry. Chop the dill leaves and stir them into the rice. Place 1 tsp of the rice in each mussel, pressing it down firmly on top of the flesh.

5 Close the mussels, bind them with kitchen twine *(above)* and place them side by side in a saucepan. Add ¼ litre water and cook the mussels over low heat for about 15 minutes, then leave them to cool in the pan.

6 Wash the lemon in hot water, and cut it into eight wedges. Wash the parsley, shake it dry and trim the stalks. Remove the kitchen twine and open the mussels. The filling and the mussel flesh should all be on one half of the shell *(above)*. Arrange the stuffed mussels on a serving dish, garnish with lemon wedges and sprigs of parsley. Serve as a starter.

Note: In Istanbul's Çiçek Pasajı district, mussel vendors move from bar to bar with trays of stuffed mussels, which customers nibble with *rakı*.

MEAT

Meat plays an important role in traditional Turkish cuisine. However, since it has always been an expensive commodity, and still is too costly for many people, it is used sparingly. The larger cuts, usually oven-roasted, are reserved mainly for special occasions such as *Kurban bayramı*, the feast of sacrifice, when family and friends share a sumptuous meal.

The everyday menu includes small quantities of lamb, veal or beef (Islam forbids the consumption of pork), which are often chopped into bite-sized pieces and cooked with vegetables, or minced for meatballs and fillings. Meat prepared on the grill, such as *şiş kebab*, is very popular; this speciality spread throughout the Balkans with the advance of the Ottoman Empire. The fame of the *döner kebab* (layers of meat turning on a large spit), spread even further and it is now a favourite fast-food snack in many parts of the world. The dish is said to have originated in the old Ottoman capital of Bursa, and is found mostly in urban areas of Turkey. Chicken, too, is widely consumed and is cooked in a variety of intriguing ways—for example, with pistachio nuts, cheese and orange juice, or aubergine purée.

In the majority of Turkish families it is the men who shop for meat. They buy it from the *kasap*, the butcher, who cuts pieces of a whole carcass to order. Meat is only rarely available pre-packed.

Lamb casserole

Easy • Summer Güveç ***Serves 4***

600 g leg or shoulder of lamb or veal
2 medium-sized onions
50 g clarified butter (see Glossary)
1 tsp tomato purée
1 tsp sweet paprika
¾ litre meat stock
6 long, pointed sweet peppers (see Glossary)
3 large tomatoes
3 small aubergines (about 500 g)
200 g green beans
3 medium-sized potatoes (about 300 g)
salt
freshly ground black pepper
30 g flat-leaf parsley

Preparation time: 45 minutes (plus 1 hour's cooking time)

2,700 kJ/640 calories per portion

1 Rinse the meat under cold running water, pat dry and cut into 3 cm cubes. Peel, quarter and slice the onions.

2 Heat 25 g of the clarified butter in a large saucepan and fry the meat over medium heat until lightly browned all over. Add the onions and stir-fry until transparent. Stir in the tomato purée and paprika. Add the stock, bring to the boil, then cover the pan and cook over medium heat for 15 minutes.

3 Preheat the oven to 180°C (350°F or Mark 4). Wash the sweet peppers and cut in half lengthwise, removing the stalks, seeds and white ribs. Rinse the pepper halves and cut the flesh into pieces. Wash and dice the tomatoes. Wash the aubergines, discarding the stalks, and chop them into fairly large chunks. Wash and trim the beans and cut them into pieces about 3 cm long. Peel, wash and slice the potatoes.

4 Using a slotted spoon, transfer the meat from the pan to a *güveç* (Turkish casserole dish) or a cast-iron pot. Arrange the vegetables in layers on top, ending with a layer of sliced potatoes. Sprinkle with a little salt and pepper. Pour in the stock. Flake the rest of the clarified butter over the top. Cover the dish or pot and cook in the centre of the oven for about 45 minutes. Wash the parsley, shake it dry and chop the leaves. Sprinkle the *güveç* with chopped parsley and serve straight from the dish.

Variation: Chicken casserole
(Piliç güveç)
Wash a small chicken weighing about 900 g, and pat dry. Cut it into joints and brown all over in a frying pan. Arrange the chicken and vegetables in layers in the *güveç*. Pour over some chicken stock and bake in the oven for about 45 minutes.

Lamb with white cabbage

Not difficult • Black Sea coast Etli lahana yemeği ***Serves 4***

600 g lamb, cut from the leg
2 medium-sized onions
40 g clarified butter (see Glossary)
1 tbsp tomato purée
salt
freshly ground black pepper
1 kg white cabbage
½ tsp hot paprika

Preparation time: 40 minutes (plus 50 minutes' cooking time)

2,200 kJ/520 calories per portion

1 Rinse the meat under cold running water, pat dry and cut into 2 cm cubes. Peel and finely chop the onions.

2 Heat the clarified butter in a large saucepan and fry the meat over high heat until the juices have evaporated and the meat is lightly browned. Add the onions and fry until they are transparent. Stir in the tomato purée and ½ litre water. Season to taste with salt and pepper, then cover and cook over low heat for about 10 minutes.

3 Trim and wash the cabbage and cut it into quarters. Remove the coarse stalks. Cut the quarters in half, then cut crosswise into strips. Stir the cabbage into the pan with the meat, adding 12.5 cl hot water if necessary.

4 Cover and cook over low heat for about 30 minutes. Add the paprika and season with salt. Serve with bread.

Note: Other types of cabbage can be substituted, if preferred.

Haricot beans with meat

Etli kurufasulye

Serves 4

250 g dried haricot beans
500 g fatty shoulder of lamb
2 medium-sized onions
2 medium-sized tomatoes
40 g clarified butter (see Glossary)
1 tbsp tomato purée
1 tsp pulbiber (flaked peppers)
50 g pastırma (cured, air-dried beef
or veal • see opposite page)
salt
freshly ground black pepper

Preparation time: 40 minutes
(plus 12 hours' soaking time
and 1 hour's cooking time)

2,700 kJ/640 calories per portion

1 Place the haricot beans in a sieve, rinse them under running water, then leave them to soak overnight in plenty of water. The next day, rinse the meat under cold running water, then cut into 2 to 3 cm cubes. Peel and finely chop the onions. Plunge the tomatoes into boiling water, leave to stand briefly, then skin them and chop the flesh.

2 Drain the beans and bring them to the boil with ¾ litre fresh water. Skim the scum from the surface. Boil the beans, uncovered, for 10 minutes, then reduce the heat and simmer for another 5 minutes. Meanwhile, in a second pan, heat the clarified butter until very hot and fry the meat until browned all over. Add the onions to the

meat and fry over medium heat until transparent. Add the tomatoes, cook them briefly with the meat and onions, then stir in the tomato purée and pulbiber.

3 Add the beans to the meat with the water in which they have been cooked. Cover the pan and cook over low heat for 40 to 45 minutes, until all the ingredients are tender. Scrape the layer of spicy paste from the outside of the *pastırma*. Cut the *pastırma* into strips, add to the pan and cook for a further 10 minutes. Season with salt and pepper. Serve with bread or rice.

Note: Pickled vegetables *(turşu)* are often served with this bean dish.

Dried meat

Preserving—a process which the Turks have turned into a culinary art form—arose out of a need to lay in stocks of food in times of plenty so that there would be enough to last them through the leaner periods.

Among their many delicious creations is *pastırma*—dried meat encased in a thick, spicy paste which, if it has been correctly hung, forms a dry outer crust. It has a strong, rather spicy smell, and a good flavour. The great advantage is that it keeps well, even in the heat of the Anatolian summers. The centre of *pastırma* production is the central Anatolian city of Kayseri.

To make *pastırma*, loin and other prime cuts of veal or beef are weighed down by stone blocks and their juices drained off. The meat is then salted and air-dried, before being smeared with a thick layer of *çemen*, a paste of cumin, fenugreek, paprika and garlic. The meat is then packed in airtight packages and stored.

Thinly sliced like salami, and served with a glass of *rakı*, *pastırma* makes a simple and tasty appetizer. It can be pan-fried with eggs, like bacon, and adds flavour to bean and chick-pea dishes. Before serving, you should remove most of the pungent paste.

In Britain, *pastırma* is available from Middle Eastern specialist food shops. If unavailable, you can substitute other types of air-dried beef such as *bresaola*, from Lombardy in Italy, or the Swiss *bündnerfleisch*.

Minced beef with spinach

Easy • Coastal regions   **Kıymalı ıspanak**   *Serves 4*

1 kg spinach
2 medium-sized onions
30 g butter
250 g minced beef
80 g long-grain rice
½ litre beef stock
½ tsp sweet paprika
allspice
freshly ground black pepper
350 g whole milk plain yogurt

Preparation time: 45 minutes
(plus 30 minutes' cooking time and 20
minutes for straining the yogurt)

1,600 kJ/380 calories per portion

1 Sort and trim the spinach, then wash and drain it, and chop coarsely. Peel and finely chop the onions.

2 Heat the butter in a saucepan or a fireproof casserole and fry the onions until transparent. Add the minced beef, breaking it into small pieces with a wooden spoon, and stir-fry over high heat until the juices evaporate and the meat is lightly browned. Reduce the heat to medium.

3 Place the rice in a sieve, rinse under cold running water, drain and stir it into the meat. Fold in the spinach and stir until it wilts. Stir in the beef stock, paprika, a little allspice and pepper. Bring to the boil, then cover and cook

over low heat for about 30 minutes. If necessary, add another 12.5 cl water so that the dish has plenty of liquid.

4 Suspend a conical sieve over a bowl and line it with a coffee filter bag. Pour in the yogurt and leave it to drain through the filter for about 20 minutes, then transfer the strained yogurt to a small serving bowl.

5 Season the meat mixture generously with salt and pepper, then serve at once, with the bowl of yogurt served separately. At the table, each person adds 1 to 2 tbsp of yogurt to the meat and spinach, and eats them together.

Meatballs in lemon sauce

Easy • Piquant   **Terbiyeli köfte**   *Serves 4*

500 g minced beef
80 g long-grain rice
2 medium-sized onions
30 g flat-leaf parsley
2 eggs
allspice
salt
freshly ground black pepper
2 tbsp flour
30 g butter
juice of 1 lemon
hot paprika

Preparation time: 30 minutes
(plus 30 minutes' cooking time)

1,900 kJ/450 calories per portion

1 Place the beef in a bowl. Place the rice in a sieve and rinse it under cold running water, then leave it to drain. Peel and very finely chop the onions. Wash the parsley, shake it dry and chop the leaves.

2 Stir the rice, one of the eggs, half the onion and half the parsley into the meat. Add a little allspice, salt and pepper, then knead thoroughly.

3 With moistened hands, take 1 tsp at a time of the meat mixture and shape it into small balls. Sift the flour into a bowl. Turn the meatballs in the flour until they are covered with a thin layer of flour. Shake off the excess.

4 Bring 1.25 litres water to the boil in a saucepan with the remaining onion, a little salt and the butter. Carefully add the meatballs, cover and cook over low heat for about 30 minutes.

5 Remove the saucepan from the heat. Whisk the lemon juice and the second egg in a bowl. Stir the egg mixture into the stock and heat through gently until the sauce starts to thicken. (Do not allow it to boil, otherwise the sauce will curdle.)

6 Add the remaining parsley to the sauce. Season with salt and pepper, and sprinkle with a little hot paprika. Serve in soup plates, with bread.

Meat-filled aubergines

More complex • Central Anatolia **Karnıyarık** *Serves 4*

4 medium-sized aubergines (about
1 kg)
5 tbsp olive oil
2 medium-sized onions
5 medium-sized tomatoes
250 g minced beef
1 tbsp tomato purée
salt
freshly ground black pepper
30 g flat-leaf parsley
2 mild or hot red chili peppers (see
Glossary)

*Preparation time: 45 minutes
(plus 30 minutes' cooking time)*

1,400 kJ/330 calories per portion

1 Wash the aubergines. Carefully peel off the leaves around the stalks, but leave the stalks on *(above)*.

2 Peel away the skins lengthwise in strips about 1 cm wide at intervals of about 1.5 cm, to create stripes on the aubergines. Make a long, deep incision in one of the peeled strips on each aubergine (to make a pocket to hold the stuffing). Dry the aubergines.

3 Preheat the oven to 180°C (350°F or Mark 4). Heat 3 tbsp of the olive oil in a frying pan and fry the aubergines for 5 to 7 minutes, until browned all over, then remove them from the pan.

4 Peel and finely chop the onions. Plunge four of the tomatoes into boiling water, leave to stand briefly, then skin and chop the flesh. Wash the fifth tomato and cut it into slices.

5 Heat the remaining 2 tbsp olive oil in the frying pan until very hot. Stir-fry the minced beef until all the juice has evaporated, breaking it up with a wooden spoon as it cooks.

6 Add the chopped onions and cook over medium heat until transparent. Add the tomato purée and the chopped tomatoes and continue to cook over low heat for about 1 minute.

7 Remove the pan from the heat and season the stuffing with salt and pepper. Wash the parsley, shake it dry, chop the leaves and stir them into the stuffing. Arrange the aubergines in a baking dish with the pockets upwards. Fill the pockets with meat stuffing and spread the rest of the stuffing over the top of the aubergines.

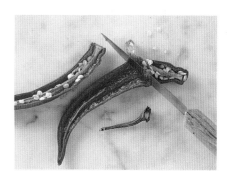

8 Wash the chili peppers, cut them in half lengthwise and remove the seeds *(above)*. Remove the stalks, if wished. Rinse the chili peppers, then place one on top of each aubergine with a slice of tomato. Pour ¼ litre water into the dish. Bake in the centre of the oven for about 30 minutes. Serve piping hot.

Wine: A full-bodied red wine such as Villa Neva, from the Aegean region, is very good with this dish.

Note: If preparing stuffed aubergines for a dinner party, you can bake them in a large roasting tin.

Stuffed peppers

Etli biber dolması

Serves 4

150 g long-grain rice
2 medium-sized onions
1 large tomato
50 g butter
30 g flat-leaf parsley
30 g dill
2 sprigs mint
400 g minced beef
allspice
salt • freshly ground black pepper
12 small, round, thin-skinned sweet
peppers (dolmalık biber)
4 small tomatoes
1 tbsp tomato purée
350 g whole milk plain yogurt

Preparation time: 45 minutes
(plus 40 minutes'
cooking time)

2,500 kJ/600 calories
per portion

1 Place the rice in a sieve, rinse and drain. Transfer the rice to a saucepan, cover with boiling water and simmer for about 15 minutes. Meanwhile, peel and finely chop the onions. Plunge the large tomato into boiling water, leave to stand briefly, then skin it and finely chop the flesh.

2 Heat 20 g of the butter in a small frying pan and sauté the onions over medium heat until transparent. Drain the cooked rice through a sieve. Wash the herbs, shake them dry, and chop finely. Place the chopped tomato, fried onions, rice, herbs and meat in a bowl with a little allspice. Season to taste with salt and pepper. Knead together thoroughly.

3 With a sharp knife, cut around the stalks of the peppers, then carefully remove the stalks, seeds and ribs. Rinse the peppers under cold running water, drain them, then stuff loosely with the meat mixture. Wash the small tomatoes and cut each of them into three slices. Use a slice of tomato as a "lid" on top of each pepper.

4 Arrange the peppers in a large pan with the "lids" upwards. Mix 37.5 cl hot water with the tomato purée and a little salt, and pour it over the stuffed peppers. Flake the rest of the butter on top, then cover and cook over low heat for about 40 minutes. Serve the peppers hot, with the yogurt.

Variations:

Use 6 peppers and 6 medium-sized firm tomatoes. Hollow out the tomatoes and fill them with the meat mixture as well. Place the stuffed tomatoes on top of the filled peppers and cook all the vegetables together.

Stuffed courgettes

(Etli kabak dolması)

Take 1.5 kg medium-sized courgettes, cut them in half and hollow out the middle of each one with a teaspoon, leaving a shell 1 cm thick. Finely chop the scooped-out flesh and mix it with the meat stuffing. Fill the courgettes and cook them in the same way as the peppers, in water with salt and butter but no tomato purée.

Meat-filled vine leaves

(Etli yaprak sarması)

Cook 250 g fresh vine leaves in briskly boiling, salted water for 1 minute (if using preserved vine leaves, boil them for 5 minutes), and spread them out on paper towels. Place 1 heaped teaspoon of meat stuffing at the stalk end of each leaf. Fold over the left and right edges to cover the stuffing, then roll the leaf towards the tip. Arrange the stuffed vine leaves in a shallow saucepan, weighing them down with an upturned plate, so that they do not unroll while cooking. Add water and a little salt and butter, cover and cook for about 30 minutes. Strain the vine leaves and serve with yogurt.

Lamb with chick-peas
Nohut

Serves 4

250 g dried chick-peas
400 fatty lamb or veal
2 medium-sized onions
2 long, pointed sweet peppers
2 medium-sized tomatoes
40 g butter
1 tbsp tomato purée
½ tsp pulbiber (flaked peppers)
freshly ground black pepper
salt
200 g sucuk (Turkish garlic sausage)
15 g flat-leaf parsley

Preparation time: 25 minutes (plus 12 hours' soaking time and 80 minutes' cooking time)

3,600 kJ/860 calories per portion

1 Pour the chick-peas into a sieve and rinse them under cold running water. Soak them overnight in plenty of water. The next day, rinse the meat under cold running water, pat it dry and cut into 2.5 cm cubes. Peel and finely chop the onions. Wash the peppers, cut them in half lengthwise and remove the stalks, seeds and white ribs. Rinse the peppers and cut them into chunks. Plunge the tomatoes into boiling water, leave to stand briefly, then skin them and finely chop the flesh.

2 Heat the butter in a saucepan or fireproof casserole and sear the meat over high heat for 7 to 8 minutes, until it is browned all over and all the juices have evaporated. Add the onions and sauté over medium heat until they are transparent. Add the tomatoes, cook briefly, then add ½ litre water and

bring to the boil. Stir in the tomato purée and *pulbiber* (flaked peppers), and season with pepper. Cover and cook over low heat for 20 minutes.

3 In another saucepan, bring the chick-peas to the boil in the water in which they have been soaking. Boil for 10 minutes, then simmer over low heat for a further 5 minutes, skimming the scum from surface. Remove the chick-peas with a slotted spoon, and add to the meat. Add the sweet peppers and, if necessary, another 12.5 cl boiling water. Cover and simmer for 35 to 40 minutes until the meat and chick-peas are tender, then season with salt.

4 Skin and slice the *sucuk*, add to the pan and cook for 5 minutes. Wash the parsley and shake it dry. Chop the leaves and stir them into the stew.

Lamb and lettuce
Kuzu kapama

Serves 4

1 kg leg of lamb
salt
2 garlic cloves
freshly ground black pepper
1 bunch spring onions
6 leaves of cos lettuce or Swiss chard
30 g butter

Preparation time: 30 minutes (plus 80 minutes' cooking time)

2,700 kJ/640 calories per portion

1 Rinse the lamb under cold running water. Half-fill a large saucepan with water. Add a little salt and bring to the boil. Add the meat and simmer over low heat for about 20 minutes, then transfer it to a fireproof casserole or pot. Reserve the stock in the saucepan.

2 Peel the garlic, then crush it finely with salt, using a pestle and mortar. Stir in plenty of pepper, then rub the meat all over with the garlic mixture. Trim and wash the spring onions, and rinse the lettuce or chard. Bring the reserved stock to the boil in the pan,

add the spring onions and lettuce or chard and cook over medium heat for about 5 minutes.

3 Remove the vegetables from the pan and drain briefly. Cover the meat in the casserole, first with the spring onions, then with the lettuce or chard. Flake the butter on top. Add ¼ litre stock, cover the casserole and cook over low heat for about 1 hour.

Note: This is a popular dish in spring, when *marul* leaves, a kind of cos lettuce, are used to cover the lamb.

Priest's ragout

Easy • Istanbul **Papaz yahnisi** *Serves 4*

800 g leg or shoulder of veal
500 g shallots
3 medium-sized tomatoes
50 g butter
2 tbsp red wine vinegar
10 cl dry red wine
1 tsp sweet paprika
½ tsp ground cinnamon
ground allspice
salt
freshly ground black pepper
2 small garlic bulbs
30 g flat-leaf parsley
cayenne pepper

**Preparation time: 40 minutes
(plus 1 hour's cooking time)**

1,400 kJ/330 calories per portion

1 Rinse the meat under cold running water, pat it dry, and cut into 3.5 cm cubes. Peel the shallots and leave them whole. Plunge the tomatoes into boiling water, leave to stand briefly, then skin them and chop the flesh.

2 Heat the butter in a high-sided frying pan and sear the meat over high heat until browned all over. Add the shallots and toss them over medium heat until transparent.

3 Add the chopped tomatoes, cook briefly, then add the vinegar, red wine and 12.5 cl water. Add the paprika,

cinnamon, a little allspice, and salt and pepper, then bring to the boil.

4 Rinse the garlic under cold running water and place, unpeeled, among the other ingredients. Cover and cook over low heat for about 30 minutes, stirring from time to time, then add 12.5 cl hot water. Cook for a further 30 minutes, until the meat is tender.

5 Wash the parsley, shake it dry, and chop the leaves. Season the ragout with salt and cayenne pepper. Sprinkle the parsley over the top and serve with *pide* (flat bread, *see page 65*).

Spices and herbs

A visit to a Turkish spice market, where myriad colours and aromas delight the eyes and nose, is a feast for the senses. Among the spices and herbs most commonly used in Turkish cuisine are black pepper, sweet and hot ground paprika, and dark red, coarsely ground, strongly flavoured flaked pepper *(pulbıber)*. These appear on the table as condiments to be sprinkled over grilled meat, as does dried oregano. In the *köftecı*, or *köfte* bars, each table has bowls of spices and herbs so customers can help themselves.

Cumin and allspice are essential ingredients in minced meat dishes; a little ground cinnamon adds a subtle

flavour to ragouts and also to rice-based stuffings for vegetables. *Sumak*, a sour, purple powder made from the berries of the vinegar shrub, is used to season bean salads and raw onions. *Çörekotu* (nigella seeds) are small black seeds with a slightly resinous taste. Mixed with sesame seeds, they are often sprinkled over

flat bread *(pide)*, or over ewe's milk cheese, to enhance the flavour.

Thyme is used with meat and stews, while fresh or dried mint is mixed with meat and rice stuffings for vegetables. It is also used to season cheese pie fillings and soups. Mint blends particularly well with fresh dill and parsley.

Adana kebabs

Adana kebabı

Takes time • Southeastern Anatolia

Serves 4

800 g minced lamb or beef
1 medium-sized onion
1 tsp pulbiber (flaked peppers)
ground cumin
freshly ground black pepper
ground allspice
salt
4 medium-sized tomatoes
8 hot or mild green chili peppers
(see Glossary)
2 tbsp olive oil
4 pide (flat bread • see page 65)
30 g flat-leaf parsley

Preparation time: 1 hour

2,100 kJ/500 calories per portion

1 Place the minced meat in a bowl. Peel the onion and finely grate it into the meat. Add the *pulbiber*, a generous amount of cumin and pepper, and a smaller amount of allspice and salt, and then thoroughly knead all the ingredients together. Leave to stand for about 10 minutes.

2 Preheat the grill. Wash and dry the tomatoes and chili peppers. Cut the tomatoes in half crosswise. Brush eight flat metal skewers, about 1 cm wide, with a little of the oil. Divide the meat mixture into eight portions. Roll each portion into a 12 to 15 cm-long sausage around one of the skewers and gently press flat. Brush the meat, the cut side of the tomatoes and the *pide* with oil.

3 Place the kebabs under the grill, surrounded by the whole chili peppers. Grill the kebabs for 5 to 6 minutes on each side. Turn the chili peppers halfway through the cooking time. Grill the tomatoes with the kebabs for the last 5 minutes, and warm the *pide* through under the grill.

4 Wash the parsley, shake it dry and trim the stalks. Cut the *pide* into strips and arrange on a serving platter. Place the kebabs, grilled vegetables and the parsley sprigs on top.

Drink: Serve the kebabs with *rakı*, diluted with iced water.

Note: These kebabs are named after the city of Adana in southern Turkey, a region well known for its scorching hot summers and fiery food.

To cool the kebabs a little, coat one half of each with tomato sauce and the other with creamy, whisked yogurt, and sprinkle all over with hot frothy butter.

Variations: Skewered rissoles
(Şiş köfte)

Knead the minced meat, grated onion and spices (omitting the *pulbiber*) with 1 egg and 1 small bread roll, soaked in water and squeezed out. Then take level tablespoons of the meat mixture and shape them into flat oval rissoles.

Thread them onto metal skewers, alternating them with tomato wedges and pieces of sweet pepper. Grill, then sprinkle with a little dried oregano.

Grilled minced meat rolls *(Köfte)*

For this popular dish, the meat is prepared as for *şiş köfte* and shaped into little rolls about the length and thickness of a thumb. Fry the rolls in 5 tbsp olive oil, or grill them on both sides. Each person seasons them to taste with dried oregano at the table. *Köfte* can be served with either rice or fried potatoes and *çoban salatası* (shepherd's salad, *see page 41*).

Shepherd's sandwiches

Çoban saç kavurması

Easy • Mediterranean coast

Serves 4

**600 g boned leg of lamb, with
a thin layer of fat
100 g shallots
2 medium-sized tomatoes
3 long, pointed, sweet peppers (see
Glossary)
150 g field mushrooms or small
button mushrooms
40 g butter
1 tsp dried thyme
salt
freshly ground black pepper
1 pide (flat bread • see page 65)
1 bunch spring onions
30 g flat-leaf parsley**

Preparation time: 45 minutes

2,000 kJ/480 calories per portion

1 Wash and dry the meat. Cut off the fat and chop it finely. Cut the meat into 1 cm cubes. Peel the shallots, cutting the larger ones in half. Plunge the tomatoes into boiling water, leave to stand briefly, then skin them and finely chop the flesh. Wash the peppers, cut them in half lengthwise and remove the stalks, seeds and white ribs. Rinse out the peppers and cut them into thin shreds. Trim the mushrooms, rinse them briefly and pat them dry.

2 Preheat the oven to 150°C (300°F or Mark 2). Heat a wok, which resembles the Turkish *saç*, or a cast-iron frying pan, until very hot. Melt the chopped fat in the hot pan. Add the meat and fry for about 10 minutes, until browned all over. Add the butter, shallots, tomatoes and peppers and stir-fry for about 1 minute. Stir in the whole mushrooms and thyme, and fry for a further 2 minutes. Reduce the heat and cook for a further 5 minutes. Season to taste with salt and pepper.

3 Place the *pide* in the centre of the oven to warm through. Trim and wash the spring onions and cut them in half lengthwise. Wash the parsley, shake it dry and trim the stalks. Cut the warm *pide* into four pieces. Cut a pocket in each and fill with the meat mixture. Arrange the parsley and spring onions on top, or serve on the side.

Note: The meat can be served with burghul wheat or rice. In Anatolia, it is eaten wrapped in very thin flat bread, known as *saç ekmeği*.

Albanian liver

Arnavut ciğeri

Easy • Istanbul

Serves 4

**4 medium-sized red onions
salt
30 g flat-leaf parsley
1 level tsp sumak (salad seasoning •
see Glossary)
600 g lamb's liver
3 tbsp flour
8 tbsp sunflower oil
freshly ground black pepper
cayenne pepper
2 medium-sized tomatoes**

Preparation time: 45 minutes

1,900 kJ/450 calories per portion

1 Peel the onions and cut them into thin rings. Sprinkle with salt, then knead thoroughly with your hands. Leave to stand for about 10 minutes, then rinse in cold water and drain thoroughly. Wash the parsley, shake it dry and finely chop the leaves. Stir them into the onions with the *sumak*.

2 Briefly rinse the liver under cold running water and pat it dry. Remove the skin and sinews, then cut it into strips about 1 cm wide and 2.5 cm long. Sift the flour on to a plate and coat the liver, shaking off any excess.

3 Heat the oil in a frying pan and fry the liver in batches over high heat for about 4 minutes, until browned all over. Drain on paper towels. Sprinkle the liver with salt, pepper and cayenne pepper, and transfer it to a warm serving dish. Arrange the onions on the side of the dish. Wash the tomatoes and then cut each of them into eight wedges. Serve the liver garnished with tomato wedges.

Note: This dish comes from the small Albanian community which settled at Arnavutköy on the Bosphorus, close to Istanbul. It can be eaten hot or warm.

Lady's thigh köfte

Kadınbudu köfte

Takes time • Tasty

Serves 4

1 large onion
50 g long-grain rice
50 g butter
salt
750 g minced beef
3 eggs
ground allspice
freshly ground black pepper
30 g flat-leaf parsley
2 tbsp flour
8 tbsp sunflower oil

For serving:
wedges of lettuce heart
sliced tomatoes
Preparation time: 45 minutes
(plus 20 minutes' cooking time, and
cooling time)

3,400 kJ/810 calories per portion

1 Peel and finely chop the onion. Place the rice in a sieve, rinse it under cold running water and drain. Heat 25 g of the butter in a saucepan and sauté the onion until transparent. Stir in the rice and continue to fry briefly. Add 20 cl water and season with salt. Cover and simmer over low heat for about 20 minutes, then leave to cool.

2 In a frying pan, fry half the minced beef in the remaining butter, breaking up the meat as it cooks. Allow the meat to cool before adding it to the rice, together with the uncooked meat and two of the eggs. Season with a little allspice, salt and plenty of pepper.

3 Wash the parsley, shake it dry and finely chop the leaves. Add them to the

meat mixture and knead thoroughly. Sift the flour on to a plate. Whisk the remaining egg in a shallow dish.

4 Heat the oil in a frying pan. Take 2 tbsp of the meat mixture at a time and shape into oval *köfte*. Coat them first in flour, then in beaten egg and fry over high heat for 2 to 3 minutes on each side, until golden-brown.

5 Transfer the *köfte* to a serving dish and serve warm or cold, with wedges of lettuce heart and sliced tomatoes.

Note: *Kadınbudu köfte* derive their unusual name from their shape.

Shish kebab

Simple • Summer Şiş kebab   *Serves 4*

600 g boned leg of lamb
1 large onion
4 tbsp virgin olive oil,
plus extra for brushing
2 tbsp lemon juice
salt
freshly ground black pepper
6 small tomatoes
8 mild or hot chili peppers (see
Glossary)
30 g flat-leaf parsley
2 tsp dried oregano

Preparation time: 1 hour
(plus 4 hours' marinating time)

2,000 kJ/480 calories per portion

1 Rinse the meat under cold running water, pat it dry and cut it into 2 cm cubes. Peel and finely grate the onion and squeeze the juice into a bowl. Stir in the 4 tbsp olive oil, the lemon juice and salt and pepper to taste. Coat the meat in the marinade, cover and leave to marinate in the refrigerator for at least 4 hours.

2 Wash the tomatoes, cut them into quarters and scrape out the seeds with a teaspoon. Wash the chili peppers and remove the stalks. Cut four of the peppers, with the seeds, crosswise into 2 cm pieces.

3 Preheat the grill. Brush eight metal skewers with oil, then thread the meat, tomatoes and chili pieces alternately on to the skewers. Arrange the whole chili peppers around the edge of the grill pan to cook with the meat. Grill the kebabs for 5 to 6 minutes on each side. Wash the parsley, shake dry and trim the stalks. Divide it between four individual plates. Place two kebabs and one grilled chili pepper on each plate, and sprinkle with oregano.

Variation: Grilled lamb chops
(Pirzola izgarası)
Marinate and then grill 8 lamb chops, trimmed so that they are easy to pick up by the bone. Cook the vegetables around the edge of the grill pan. Sprinkle the meat with oregano. Serve with *pide* (flat bread, *see page 65*), brushed lightly with oil and warmed under the grill. The chops may be eaten with whole spring onions or a salad.

Chicken in aubergine purée

Beğendili piliç

Serves 4

1 kg small aubergines
juice of 1 lemon
80 g butter
1 heaped tbsp flour
37.5 cl milk
3 tbsp freshly grated kaşar or
emmenthal cheese
salt
1 oven-ready chicken (about 1.2 kg)
3 large tomatoes
3 shallots
½ tsp dried thyme
freshly ground black pepper
30 g flat-leaf parsley

**Preparation time: 45 minutes
(plus 30 minutes for roasting the
aubergines, and 50 minutes'
cooking time)**

3,100 kJ/740 calories per portion

1 Preheat the oven to 250°C (450°F or Mark 8). Wash and dry the aubergines, then roast them in the centre of the oven for 20 to 30 minutes, until the skin is brown and wrinkled. Rinse the aubergines briefly in cold water, and peel them, starting at the stalk end. Cut them in half and scrape out the dark-coloured seeds. Chop the flesh very finely, place it in a bowl, sprinkle with lemon juice, and reserve.

2 Heat 30 g butter in a saucepan and cook the flour until lightly browned. Using a hand whisk, vigorously stir in the chopped aubergine. Add the milk a little at a time and bring to the boil, stirring constantly. Simmer over low heat for about 2 minutes, until the mixture thickens, then remove from the heat. Stir in the cheese and 20 g of the butter. Season the purée with salt.

3 Wash the chicken, pat it dry and divide into eight joints. Plunge the tomatoes into boiling water, leave to stand briefly, then skin them and finely chop the flesh. Peel the shallots. Heat the remaining butter in a frying pan and fry the chicken over high heat for about 10 minutes on each side, until lightly browned. Transfer to a plate.

4 Fry the shallots in the fat remaining in the pan, until transparent. Add the tomatoes and continue to cook over medium heat for about 3 minutes. Add ¼ litre water, bring to the boil, then add the thyme. Season with salt and pepper. Add the chicken, cover and cook over low heat for 30 minutes. Heat the purée and divide it between four plates. Arrange the chicken joints and sauce on top. Wash the parsley, shake dry and use to garnish the dish.

Chicken and pistachio rolls

Piliç sarması

Serves 4

4 boned chicken breasts (about
400 g)
salt • freshly ground black pepper
100 g shelled pistachio nuts
50 g young kaşar cheese (see
Glossary)
1 egg white
3 tbsp sunflower oil
1 tsp flour • juice of 2 oranges
cayenne pepper
4 orange slices for garnish

Preparation time: 45 minutes

1,600 kJ/380 calories per portion

1 Wash the chicken breasts and pat dry. Lay them flat on a chopping board and slice them crosswise through the middle with a sharp knife, to make eight thin slices. Sprinkle lightly with salt and pepper.

2 Finely chop half the pistachio nuts in a food processor and sprinkle them over the chicken. Cut the cheese into eight thin slices and lay them on top of the chicken. Roll up the chicken slices and secure the ends of the rolls with wooden skewers. Whisk the egg white in a shallow bowl. Coarsely chop the

remaining pistachio nuts and spread them on a plate. Dip the chicken rolls in the egg white and then coat them in the chopped pistachio nuts, pressing the nuts firmly into the meat.

3 Heat the oil in a frying pan and fry the chicken rolls over medium heat for 8 to 10 minutes. Remove from the pan and keep warm. Brown the flour in the oil, then add the orange juice and bring briefly to the boil. Season lightly with salt and cayenne pepper. Pour the sauce over the chicken and serve, garnished with halved orange slices.

PASTRIES AND DESSERTS

A ngel's hair dessert is typical of the rich array of Turkish cakes, sweet pastries and desserts, all of them as mouthwatering as their names are enchanting. They have their origins in the refined cuisine of the Sultan's Palace in Istanbul, where an army of specialist cooks strove to create ever more elaborate titbits with which to tempt the Sultan's harem. Today, they are displayed to great effect on large trays in the windows of the specialist baklava shops, where the age-old craft is still practised.

Less elaborate sweetmeats were developed by the ordinary citizens of Turkey: delicious halva made from sesame seeds or wheat, with almonds and pistachio nuts, rice-flour puddings, and fresh or dried fruit desserts. One sugary snack that can be enjoyed at any time is *reçel* (fruit boiled down in syrup to a jam-like consistency). But probably the most famous sweet of all is *lokum* or "Turkish Delight", which Turks like to offer to their guests, perhaps with a glass of chilled water or Turkish coffee. Sweets are rarely eaten at the end of a meal, but as a between-meals snack.

This chapter includes recipes for both complicated and easy-to-make everyday sweets. Because making some of them is quite a skilled operation, many people prefer to buy items such as *baklava* ready-made.

Filo pastry slices

Baklava

Needs care • Traditional

Serves 8 to 10

For the pastry:
1 kg flour • 4 eggs
4 cl sunflower oil
salt
200 g cornflour

For the filling:
200 g coarsely ground hazelnuts
3 tbsp icing sugar
10 tbsp sunflower oil

For the syrup:
300 g sugar
juice of 1 lemon

For sprinkling:
50 g coarsely ground hazelnuts

Preparation time: 3 hours
(plus 2½ hours' standing time,
and 30 minutes' cooking time)

3,900 kJ/930 calories per portion
(if serving 10)

1 Sift the flour on to a work surface and make a deep well in the middle. Break the eggs into the well, then pour in the oil. Measure 2.25 cl cold water into a jug. Pour one third of the water into the well. Sprinkle 1 tsp salt over the flour. Using a spatula, mix the ingredients in the well, and stir in some of the flour from the edge. Add the rest of the water a little at a time, stirring in more flour, then knead all the ingredients together to create an elastic dough.

2 With the palms of your hands and the balls of your thumbs, knead the dough, stretching it backwards and forwards, for about 10 minutes, then stretch into a roll about 60 cm long. Fold the two ends crosswise one on top of the other, and tuck them under the middle. Cover the dough with a damp cloth and leave to stand for 20 minutes.

3 Stretch the dough lengthwise and knead it vigorously with the balls of your thumbs. Shape it again into a roll, cover with the damp cloth and leave to stand for a further 20 minutes. Repeat this process twice more, then shape into a smooth roll about 2.5 cm thick. Cut it into 22 equal-sized pieces.

4 Pile a little cornflour at the edge of the work surface. Working with two pieces of dough at once (one in each hand), gently flatten them with your palms into circles 8 to 9 cm in diameter, thicker in the middle of the circle, becoming thinner towards the edges. Dredge lightly with cornflour, lay one on top of the other and gently press flat. Place the lower circle on top and repeat the process. Shape all the pastry in the same way. Leave to stand under a damp cloth for 20 minutes.

5 Roll out each circle to a larger circle about 20 cm in diameter, rolling from the centre outwards so it is thicker in

the centre. Sift the cornflour over both sides of the pastry circles. Make three stacks of pastry circles and cover with a damp cloth. Leave to stand for about 45 minutes. To make the filling, mix the nuts and icing sugar with 5 tbsp water.

6 To roll out the pastry (*yufka*), use an oriental rolling pin and a large pastry board (preferably marble). Brush off the damp cornflour from one pastry circle and sprinkle with dry cornflour. Roll the pastry outwards from the middle, first with a conventional rolling pin, then stretch it with the *oklava* to a circle about 60 cm in diameter. To do this, place the *oklava* slightly in from the edge of the pastry. Lift the pastry edge over the *oklava* and roll up the pastry towards the middle. Without rolling, pull the pastry backwards and forwards four or five times to stretch it, with the help of the *oklava*. Unroll the pastry completely and repeat the same process with another section of the edge, continuing until the pastry is the

desired size. Repeat with all the sheets then lay them one on top of the other. It is important to change the order of the sheets, by turning over the pile. To prevent the pastry you have prepared first from drying out as you do the rest, fold the first one-third of the sheets in four and place them flat in a plastic bag until all the pastry is ready to use.

7 Preheat the oven to 200°C (400°F or Mark 6). Line a 30 to 32 cm round tin with greaseproof paper brushed with oil. Brush the cornflour off three pastry sheets and sprinkle with oil. Lay them in the tin, with the edges overhanging. Cut nine sheets to the same size as the tin and brush off the cornflour. Brush the sheets with oil and lay them one on top of the other in the tin. Spread the filling on top. Fold the overhanging edges inwards.

8 Cut another eight sheets to the size of the tin, brush off the cornflour and lay two of them on top of the filling,

without brushing with oil. Brush the other six with oil and lay them one on top of the other. Remove the cornflour from the last two sheets, brush with oil and lay them on top of the others, then, using the back of a knife, carefully push them down around the edge of the tin. Cut the *baklava* into 4 cm wide strips, then cut into diamond shapes. Sprinkle with the rest of the oil, then bake in the oven, one shelf up from the bottom, for 30 minutes.

9 Meanwhile make the syrup. Boil the sugar with 20 cl water, uncovered, over high heat for about 2 minutes. Stir in the lemon juice. Pour the hot, thin syrup over the *baklava*, as soon as it comes out of the oven. Leave it to cool in the tin, then sprinkle with the nuts.

Variation: *Baklava* can also be filled with coarsely ground pistachio nuts or walnuts, instead of hazelnuts.

Angel's hair dessert

Künefe

125 g sugar
1 tbsp lemon juice
250 g tel kadayıfı (fresh angel's hair pastry • see Note)
60 g butter, plus extra for greasing
100 g dil peyniri or mozzarella cheese
2 tbsp chopped pistachio nuts

Preparation time: 45 minutes (plus 20 minutes' cooking time)

2,300 kJ/550 calories per portion

1 First make a light syrup. Bring the sugar and 12.5 cl water to the boil in a saucepan. Add the lemon juice and cook, uncovered, over medium heat for about 10 minutes. Leave to cool.

2 Lay the angel's hair pastry strands between two damp cloths and leave for about 15 minutes to make them more pliable.

3 Preheat the oven to 200°C (400°F or Mark 6). Grease four small baking dishes about 12 cm in diameter, or four ovenproof dessert plates, with butter. Divide the pastry into eight equal piles and place one of them in each dish. Melt the 60 g butter and, using a large brush, dot the four portions of pastry in the dishes with half the melted butter. Dice the cheese and sprinkle it over the pastry. Cover the cheese with the rest of the pastry strands, press down firmly and brush with the remaining butter.

4 Bake in the centre of the oven for about 20 minutes, until brown. Pour the syrup over the hot desserts, leave to soak in for 30 seconds, then sprinkle with the chopped nuts, and serve hot.

Note: Angel's hair pastry, also known as *kataıfı* or *kadaıf* pastry, is made by pouring a flour and water batter through a sieve onto a hot metal tray to produce long strands like shredded wheat. It is sold in Greek or Middle Eastern specialist food shops.

Wedding rice

Zerde

Takes time • Central Anatolia

Serves 4 to 6

125 g pudding rice
1 g saffron threads or ground saffron
200 g sugar
1 tbsp cornflour
50 g pine-nuts
1 ripe red pomegranate
50 g raisins
2 tbsp rose water

Preparation time: 1 hour (plus 30 minutes' cooking time)

1,300 kJ/310 calories per portion (if serving 6)

1 Place the rice in a sieve, rinse under cold running water and drain. Soak the saffron in 3 tbsp hot water for about 5 minutes. Bring the rice to the boil with 1.25 litres water and the sugar. Once it has come to the boil, cover the rice and cook over low heat for about 25 minutes.

2 Stir the saffron and water into the rice. Dissolve the cornflour in a little cold water. Using a hand whisk, stir the cornflour mixture into the cooked rice and return to the boil. Continue to stir until the rice thickens. If it becomes too thick, stir in another 12.5 cl water and briefly return to the boil.

3 Divide the rice between four to six small dessert bowls. Lightly toast the pine-nuts in a dry frying pan over low heat for about 3 minutes, then leave to cool. Using a sharp knife, make an incision round the pomegranate about 3 cm away from the stem end, then remove the shell like a lid. Starting at the top, make four cuts in the fruit, and break off the pieces. Scoop the sweet seeds from the bitter pith. Wash the raisins in hot water and pat them dry.

4 Decorate each portion of rice with raisins, pine-nuts and pomegranate seeds, making either stripes or a star pattern. Sprinkle with a little rose water before serving.

Note: This rice dessert is traditionally served cold at Turkish weddings, as the name suggests.

Semolina halva

More difficult · All regions

İrmik helvası

Serves 6

175 g butter
225 g semolina
100 g slivered almonds
1 litre milk
300 g sugar
1 tsp ground cinnamon
3 tbsp shelled pistachio nuts
3 tbsp pine-nuts

Preparation time: 1 hour
(plus cooling time)

3,400 kJ/810 calories per serving

1 Heat the butter in a wide-based pan. Add the semolina and slivered almonds, and stir-fry them over medium heat for 15 to 20 minutes, until both the nuts and the semolina are golden. Remove the pan from the heat.

2 In a second pan, heat the milk and sugar, then pour the milk over the hot semolina and almonds, taking care as the mixture may spit. Return the pan to the heat and simmer over medium heat for 10 to 15 minutes, stirring until the mixture is thick and firm.

3 Rinse out a small, square baking tin with cold water. Pour the halva mixture into the wet tin and smooth the surface with a spoon dipped in water. Allow the halva to cool, then leave it to chill in the refrigerator for about 1 hour.

4 Carefully turn the *halva* out on to a serving dish. Sprinkle the cinnamon on top, making stripes or a pattern of your choice. Coarsely chop the pistachio nuts, then decorate the halva with the pistachio nuts and the pine-nuts. Serve it cut into slices.

Note: *Halva* is one of Turkey's most ancient sweetmeats. It is made when visitors are expected, or for religious festivals, such as *Şeker Bayrami* (the Sugar Feast at the end of Ramadan), or for circumcision celebrations.

Fried pastries with syrup

Time consuming · Traditional

Tulumba tatlısı

Makes about 30

For the syrup:
350 g sugar
juice of ½ lemon

For the dough:
70 g semolina
180 g plain flour
1 tbsp sugar
20 g butter · salt
4 eggs
25 g cornflour
1 litre sunflower oil for deep-frying

For sprinkling:
2 tbsp finely chopped pistachio nuts

Preparation time: 1½ hours

880 kJ/210 per calories per pastry

1 First make a light syrup. Bring the sugar and ½ litre water to the boil in a saucepan. Add the lemon juice, then cook, uncovered, over medium heat for about 10 minutes. Leave the syrup to cool in the pan.

2 Meanwhile, mix the semolina and the flour in a bowl. Over high heat, bring ¼ litre water to the boil with the sugar, butter and a little salt. Reduce the heat. Add the semolina and flour all at once. Stir constantly for about 10 minutes, until the dough comes away from the bottom of the pan in a large ball.

3 Transfer the dough to a bowl and stir in the eggs and cornflour to create a smooth, glutinous consistency. Heat the oil in an electric deep-fryer or a high-sided pan, until small bubbles rise from a wooden chopstick dipped in the oil.

4 Fill an icing bag fitted with a large, serrated nozzle with the dough. Holding the icing bag over the pan, squeeze out about 4 to 5 cm of dough, snip it with kitchen scissors, and drop it into the hot oil, taking care as it may spit. Fry strips of dough in batches until they are lightly browned.

5 Remove the pastries from the pan with a slotted spoon and drain them briefly on paper towels. Leave them in the syrup for about 5 minutes so they are soaked through. Serve as soon as possible, sprinkled with pistachio nuts.

Yogurt cake

Quick and easy • Traditional

Yoğurt tatlısı

Serves 8 to 10

500 g whole-milk plain yogurt
4 eggs
700 g sugar
1 vanilla pod
125 g butter plus extra for greasing the cake tin
breadcrumbs for lining the cake tin
20 g baking powder
500 g semolina
juice of 1 lemon
50 g grated fresh or dessicated coconut

Preparation time: 30 minutes (plus 45 minutes' cooking time, and cooling time)

2,600 kJ/620 calories per portion (if serving 10)

1 Pour the yogurt into a bowl. Add the eggs, 200 g of the sugar and the pulp from the vanilla pod. Melt the butter in a small frying pan and leave it to cool. Meanwhile, preheat the oven to 180°C (350°F or Mark 4). Grease the cake tin with butter and sprinkle the inside with breadcrumbs.

2 Add the cooled butter to the yogurt and stir thoroughly with a hand whisk until the sugar has dissolved. Stir the baking powder into the semolina, then sift the mixture into the yogurt and mix to a dough. Transfer the cake mixture to the tin and bake in the centre of the oven for about 45 minutes.

3 Meanwhile, make a light syrup. Bring the remaining 500 g sugar and ¾ litre water to the boil in a saucepan. Add the lemon juice and cook, uncovered, over high heat for about 5 minutes. Leave the syrup until cold.

4 Leave the cake to cool for about 1 minute, then stand the tin on a large dish and gradually pour all the syrup over the cake. Leave it until cold, then cut into squares in the tin. Serve on a cake dish, sprinkled with the coconut.

Note: The sharp flavour of the yogurt offsets the sweetness of the syrup.

"Pan scrapings"

More difficult • All regions

Kazandibi

Serves 4

1 litre milk
150 g sugar
160 g rice flour
1 vanilla pod
30 g butter
40 g icing sugar
1 tbsp rose water
2 tsp ground cinnamon

Preparation time: 45 minutes
(plus cooling time)

2,300 kJ/550 calories per portion

1 Pour the milk into a saucepan. Mix the sugar, rice flour and the pulp from the vanilla pod, then stir them into the milk. Add the empty vanilla pod. Heat the milk, stirring constantly. Keep it on the boil for 2 to 3 minutes. Remove the vanilla pod, then leave to stand briefly.

2 Grease a square, flat, heavy-bottomed, fireproof dish (not non-stick), 26 cm in diameter *(see Note, below)*, with the butter and sprinkle evenly with the icing sugar. Pour the pudding into the dish and smooth the surface. Turn the largest burner on the hob to maximum.

3 Place the dish on the burner and turn it down to medium. Leave it standing on the heat for about 10 minutes, until it gives off a caramel smell, turning the dish from time to time so that the bottom of the pudding browns evenly. Leave the pudding to cool in the dish for about 20 minutes.

4 Cut the pudding into quarters. Using a spatula, carefully lift out the pieces and place them on four dessert plates, then roll them up with the brown side showing.

5 Sprinkle the rolls with rose water and then with cinnamon in a diagonal stripe pattern. Serve cold.

Note: You can use a frying pan to make this pudding, but bear in mind that the resulting quarters will be triangular, not square-shaped.

Noah's pudding

Aşure

Serves 4 to 6

125 g whole wheat
100 g dried haricot beans
100 g dried chick-peas
6 dried figs • 100 g dried apricots
100 g currants • 100 g raisins
3 oranges
300 g sugar • 1 tbsp cornflour
2 tbsp rose water
2 tsp ground cinnamon
1 pomegranate
150 g coarsely chopped walnuts

Preparation time: 2 hours
(plus 12 hours' soaking time,
and up to 5 hours' cooking time)

3,200 kJ/760 calories per portion
(if serving 6)

1 Rinse the wheat, haricot beans and chick-peas separately in a sieve, then soak them separately overnight in plenty of cold water. Soak the figs and apricots in water for 4 to 5 hours. The following day, drain the wheat and cook in fresh water in a covered pan over low heat for 3 to 4 hours, until tender. Cook the haricot beans and chick-peas in separate pans for 40 to 50 minutes. Drain the wheat, beans and chick-peas. Drain and finely chop the figs and the apricots. Wash and drain the currants and raisins separately. Peel all the oranges and divide them into segments.

2 Cook the wheat, beans, chick-peas, figs, apricots, currants and oranges

with the sugar and 1 litre water over low heat for about 20 minutes. Dissolve the cornflour in a little water, stir it into the pudding and return to the boil.

3 Stir the rose water and cinnamon into the pudding, then spoon it into individual dessert bowls and leave to cool. Cut the pomegranate in half and scoop out the seeds. Serve the pudding cold, decorated with raisins, walnuts and pomegranate seeds.

Note: Noah is said to have invented this dish after he landed on Mount Ararat in eastern Anatolia. As the flood waters subsided, he took all the food he still had in store and made it into a pudding.

Quinces in syrup

Ayva tatlısı

Serves 4

4 large, ripe quinces
250 g sugar
juice of 1 lemon
4 cloves
5 cm piece cinnamon stick
100 g kaymak (see Glossary) or
double cream
1 tsp ground cinnamon

Preparation time: 30 minutes
(plus 1 hour's cooking time)

1,800 kJ/430 calories per portion

1 Preheat the oven to 200°C (400°F or Mark 6). Peel and halve the quinces and scoop out the cores with a sharp-edged spoon. Mix the sugar with ½ litre water in a saucepan and bring to the boil. Add the lemon juice, cloves and cinnamon stick and return to the boil. Add the quince halves, cover and simmer over medium heat for about 10 minutes.

2 Place the quinces side by side in a round, high-sided baking dish and pour half the syrup over them. Bake in the centre of the oven for about 1 hour, until they are tender and have turned a reddish colour, sprinkling the quinces with the rest of the juice from time to time. Leave to cool, then cover the dish and chill in the refrigerator.

3 Before serving, remove the quince halves from the juice, drain them briefly, then arrange them, cut side up, on individual dessert plates. Fill each half with 1 tsp *kaymak* or double cream and top with 2 to 3 tbsp of the quince syrup. Sprinkle each with a little ground cinnamon.

Variation: Pumpkin in syrup

(Balkabağı tatlısı)
Peel a 1.5 kg pumpkin and remove the seeds and pulp. Cut the flesh into chunks, then mix with 500 g sugar and leave overnight to draw off the juice. Simmer the fruit, covered, in its own juice for about 40 minutes. Sprinkle the cooked chunks of fruit with juice and top with chopped walnuts.

Bergamot jam

Turunç reçeli

3 to 4 large, unwaxed bergamots (see Glossary) or Seville oranges
juice of ½ lemon
1 kg sugar
1 tsp citric acid (limontuzu • see Glossary)

Preparation time: 2 hours (plus a total of 2 hours spread over several days)

5,000 kJ/1,200 calories per jar

1 Wash the bergamots in hot water and wipe dry. Gently grate the rind of each one with a fine grater. Using a sharp knife, score the rind at 2 cm intervals, starting at the stalk end and finishing at the opposite end. Carefully peel off the rind in strips and place in cold water with the lemon juice.

2 Thread a needle with a long piece of strong white thread. Roll up each strip, then sew the rolls together to make two round garlands. Place them in cold water for about 30 minutes, then drain. Bring a large pan of water to the boil. Place the garlands in the water and boil over medium heat for 30 minutes, then drain. Soak them in cold water for four days, changing the water each day.

3 Unthread the rolls of rind and place them in a saucepan. Add the sugar and ¼ litre water. Stir and leave to stand until the sugar has dissolved. Cover and simmer over low heat for about 1 hour. About 5 minutes before the end of the cooking time, stir in the *limontuzu*. Leave the jam to cool in the pan, before filling and sealing the jars.

Variation: Fig jam *(İncir reçeli)*
Wash and dry 1 kg figs, and cut each fig into quarters. Cover with 1 kg sugar and leave overnight to draw off the juice. Place in a pan with the juice of 1 lemon. Simmer over low heat for about 1 hour. Transfer the jam to jars while still hot, then seal.

Reçel

This home-made preserve is not simply a kind of jam, to be spread on freshly baked bread and enjoyed for breakfast; in Turkey, it is considered a sweet delicacy worthy of offering to guests. Most *reçel* comes from the major fruit-growing regions located around the Sea of Marmara, inland from the Aegean, and along the Mediterranean coast.

Turkish cooks devote a great deal of time to preserving fruit, and the *reçel*-making season extends right through from spring to autumn. The most popular fruits for preserving are strawberry, sour cherry, peach, apricot, plum, apple and quince.

To make *reçel*, the fruit is first covered in sugar to draw off the juice. It is then removed from the juice, which is boiled to make a syrup. The fruit is then returned to the syrup and gently simmered. An oriental note may be added with flavourings such as rose petals, small figs or bergamot rind. It is the strong, aromatic, slightly bitter taste of bergamot oil—used mainly for perfumery—which gives earl grey tea its characteristic tang.

Suggested Menus

The Turks are fiercely proud of their national cuisine, and are particularly attached to their traditional dishes, which perhaps explains why Turkish cuisine has scarcely been influenced by that of other lands and meals are still cooked as they have been for generations. The day begins with a breakfast *(kahvaltı)* of flat bread *(pide)*, long white loaves *(francola)* or sesame rings *(simit)*, with cheese, olives, tomato, cucumber, hard-boiled eggs and *reçel*, a type of jam. Soup is a popular fortifier in rural areas. Bread is served at every meal to accompany each course.

Lunch *(öğle yemeği)* is kept simple—perhaps just something left over from the previous day. The main meal of the day is dinner *(akşam yemeği)*, comprising several hot and cold dishes which vary according to the time of year. Sometimes all the food will be brought to the table at the same time, or the hot dishes will be brought on after the cold ones have been finished. In the south of Turkey, food is seldom eaten piping hot, but is left to cool for a while first. Fresh or stewed fruit is usually offered for dessert. The meal ends with the customary small cup of strong Turkish coffee *(kahve)* or tea *(çay)* in a tulip-shaped glass.

In rural areas, the dining table is often a simple round wooden board which is mounted on low, folding trestles and a tablecloth spread on top just before the meal is ready to be served. The family sits cross-legged on cushions, and each person takes a corner of the cloth, or spreads the edge of it over their lap, to use as a napkin.

In town and country alike, Turkish hospitality is difficult to refuse. If visitors turn up unexpectedly, it goes without saying that they are invited to share the meal. Those who call outside meal times will be offered tea or coffee and a pastry or sweetmeat, kept in reserve for such occasions.

Everyday menus

Ezo, the bride's soup	33
Green beans with tomato	79
Cheese-filled börek	62
Minced beef with spinach	107
Fresh fruit in season	—
Cucumber salad with yogurt	40
Chick-pea purée	48
Stuffed vine leaves	80
Shepherd's salad	41
Skewered rissoles (variation)	117
Fresh fruit in season	—
Red lentil soup	30
Carrot salad (variation)	42
Aubergine salad (with cubed ewe's milk cheese)	46
Shepherd's sandwiches	119
Fresh fruit in season	—

Okra in olive oil	74
Stuffed aubergines	85
Herby cheese dip	45
Meatballs in lemon sauce	107
Fresh fruit in season	—

Quick menus

Alpine soup	26
Shepherd's salad	41
Cigarette böreks	66
Skewered lamb	121
Fresh fruit in season	—
Cucumber salad with yogurt	40
Courgette fritters	45
Fried aubergines	51
Grilled ocean perch	92
Fresh fruit in season	—
Pan-fried cheese pasties	71
Carrot salad (variation)	42
Albanian liver	119
Fresh fruit in season	—
Green pea soup	28
Herby cheese dip	45
Shepherd's salad	41
Lady's thigh köfte	120
Fresh fruit in season	—

Menus to prepare in advance

Red lentil soup	30
Burghul salad (with ewe's milk cheese)	46 —
Aubergine salad	46
Stuffed peppers	110
Fresh fruit in season	—
Bean salad	51
Stuffed vine leaves	80
Turkish ravioli	68
Shepherd's salad	41
Quinces in syrup	134

Vegetarian menus

Poached eggs in yogurt sauce	37
Carrot salad (variation)	42
Chick-pea purée	48
Cheese-filled börek	62
Fresh fruit in season	—

Okra in olive oil	74
Courgette fritters	45
Herby cheese dip	45
Winter vegetable hotpot	83
Fresh fruit in season	—

Menus with meat

Wedding soup	28
Stuffed peppers	110
Shepherd's salad	41
Grilled lamb chops (variation)	121
Fresh fruit in season	—

Ezo, the bride's soup	33
Turkish-style pizzas	65
Carrot salad (variation)	42
Meatballs in lemon sauce	107
Fresh fruit in season	—

Tarhana soup	34
Albanian liver	119
Green beans with tomato	79
Adana kebabs	116
Fresh fruit in season	—

Menus with fish

Grey mullet with olive oil	95
Shepherd's salad	41
Sea bass parcels	90
Carrot salad (variation)	42
Fresh fruit in season	—

Mussels with walnut sauce	96
Burghul salad	46
Courgette fritters	45
Baked red mullet	95
Fresh fruit in season	—

Dinner party menu

Aubergine salad	46
(with a few cubes of ewe's milk cheese)	—
Stuffed vine leaves	80
Herby cheese dip	45
Swordfish kebabs	89
Shepherd's salad	41
Priest's ragout	114
Fresh fruit in season	—
Fried pastries with syrup	131

Spring menu

Broad beans in olive oil	82
Purslane in yogurt sauce	42
Cigarette böreks	66
Lamb and lettuce	113
Fresh fruit in season	—

Summer menu

Cucumber salad with yogurt	40
Green beans with tomato	79
(with ewe's milk cheese)	—
Sardines in vine leaves	88
Shepherd's salad	41
Fresh fruit in season	—

Autumn menu

Wedding soup	28
Leeks in olive oil	77
Haricot beans with meat	104
Pickled peppers	54
Fresh fruit in season	—

Winter menu

Red lentil soup	30
Borlotti beans in olive oil	79
Shepherd's salad	41
Lady's thigh köfte	120
Pumpkin in syrup	134

Rakı table for 8 to 10

A *rakı sofrası* consists of a number of cold and warm dishes (the cold dishes being served first), traditionally accompanied by raki or wine. The menu might include:

Ewe's milk cheese, tomatoes, cucumbers and olives	—
Aubergine salad	46
Herby cheese dip	45
Chick-pea purée	48
Pink princess salad	42
Mother-in-law's köfte	60
Pickled peppers	54
Circassian chicken	52
Stuffed vine leaves	80
Shepherd's salad	41
Stuffed mussels	99
Albanian liver	119
Cigarette böreks	66
Prawn gratin	96

Glossary

This glossary is intended as a brief guide to some less familiar cookery terms and ingredients, including Turkish words or items found on menus.

Adaçayı: herb tea, brewed from the leaves, and occasionally flowers, of sage. A refreshing summer or winter drink enjoyed at any time of day in Turkey.

Arabica *(coffea arabica var mocca)*: a strong, spicy variety of coffee originating from Arabia, the home of coffee. It is ground from small beans and used to make Turkish coffee.

Ayran: a refreshing summer drink made with two parts chilled, sour, plain yogurt, one part cold water, and a little salt, whisked by hand just before serving. It is good with meals, but is also drunk by itself at any time of the day.

Baklavacı: *baklava* baker.

Bergamot: a small bitter citrus fruit, similar to a Seville orange, whose rind is added to make the popular jam *reçel*.

Beyaz peynir: ewe's milk cheese preserved in brine and sold in blocks.

Beyaz şarap: white wine.

Bonito: a warm-water tuna fish about 80 cm long, with four to seven dark stripes on its silvery underside. Known as *palamut* in Turkish.

Börek: a savoury pastry made from *yufka*, thin ready-made sheets of pastry, or pre-cooked pasta dough.

Börekçi: *börek* baker.

Burghul: cooked, cracked wheat, available coarsely ground *(kalın bulgur)* or finely ground *(köftelik bulgur* or *simit bulgur)*. See also page 60.

Çay: Turkish black tea, prepared in two pots stacked one on top of the other. A strong infusion of tea leaves and water is brewed in the slightly smaller upper pot, while the lower one is filled with boiling water. The infusion is poured into a glass and diluted to taste with boiling water.

The tea has a light fragrant flavour which is very refreshing, and the Turks drink it throughout the day.

Çemen: spices mixed to a paste and used to coat *pastırma,* an air-dried meat.

Chili peppers: fiery, long, thin, dark green or red peppers, known as *acibiber* in Turkey. They contain volatile oils that can irritate the skin and eyes, and must be handled with caution. Wash hands immediately after using them.

Citric acid: acid which occurs naturally in citrus fruit. Commercially produced citric acid is sold in powder or granular crystals and is used mainly for preserving soft fruit drinks, in home wine making, and to help produce a good set in jam.

Clarified butter: butter clarified so that it can be used for frying at higher temperatures. To clarify butter, heat until melted and all bubbling stops. Remove from the heat and stand until the sediment has sunk to the bottom, then gently pour off the fat, straining it through muslin. Chill and use as required.

Çorba: soup.

Çorbacı: soup cook.

Çörekotu: nigella seeds, also known (incorrectly) as onion seeds. Small and black, with a resinous taste, they are the seeds of a kind of buttercup. They are sprinkled over *pide* (flat bread) and savoury pastries, and are also a tasty addition to ewe's milk cheese.

Cornelian cherries: called *kızılcık* in Turkish, these delicately sharp, red, olive-shaped cherries, about 2 cm long, are the fruit of a wild shrub. When ripe, they are made into jam and the juice is used to make *şerbet*.

Cumin: spice from a Mediterranean plant, known as *kimyon* in Turkey. Popular throughout the orient, cumin is most commonly used in Turkish cuisine to season minced meat dishes, *hummus* and Turkish pizza.

Dil peyniri: the name literally means "tongue cheese". This stringy-textured

cheese is unsalted and melts well. It is also used to make *künefe*, angel's hair dessert *(recipe, page 128)*.

Dolmalık biber: small, round, thin-skinned sweet peppers, delicious eaten stuffed and also very good for pickling.

Döner kebab: layers of thinly-sliced meat and slabs of minced meat marinated in onion juice and spices, cooked on a rotating spit.

Elmaçayı: tea that is brewed from dried, chopped, apple peel. It makes a refreshing drink at any time of day. Instant *elmaçayi* is sold in jars.

Flaked peppers: *see Pulbiber.*

Helvacı: Turkish maker of *halva,* the sesame-seed sweetmeat pressed into blocks, then served in slices.

Izgara: grilled.

Kadayıfçı: *tel kadayif* (angel's hair pastry) maker.

Kahve: Turkish coffee, made and served in an individual copper or aluminium, long-handled coffee pot called a *cezve*. See also page 23.

Kahvalti: breakfast.

Kandil rings *(kandil simidi)*: small shortcrust pastry rings, sprinkled with sesame seeds. These traditional pastries are made for certain religious feasts.

Kaşar cheese *(kaşar peyniri)*: semi-hard cheese made from cow's or ewe's milk, or a mixture of the two, usually produced in large wheels. The flavour varies according to age, from mild and slightly salty to piquant, even rather pungent. The finest *kaşar peyniri* comes from the countryside around Kars in eastern Anatolia. The Afyon, Eskişehir and Edirne regions also produce high quality cheese. Specialist Turkish shops sell very young *kasar* cheese in small discs or blocks sealed in foil. This cheese is similar to *kaskaval*, which is produced in the Balkans, and the Greek cheese, *kasseri*.

Kaymak: cream skimmed off the top of boiled milk and reduced until thick and almost firm enough to cut. It is served as a dessert with fresh strawberries or honey. Double cream or *mascarpone* are both good substitutes.

Kebab: meat, usually cut into large or small cubes, and cooked on a skewer over a charcoal grill (or, nowadays, just as likely to be cooked by gas or electricity). Cooking meat on skewers over a fire was the traditional cooking method used by the nomadic tribes, who had to live off the land as they travelled, and prepare meals without using cooking pots.

Kırmızı şarap: red wine.

Kuş üzümü: translated literally as "bird currants", these tiny currants are added to rice dishes and rice-based stuffings for vegetables.

Limontuzu: literally "lemon salt". *See* Citric acid.

Lion's milk: nickname for *rakı*, the spirit which turns milky white when diluted with water.

Long, pointed sweet peppers: larger than chili peppers, usually mild and pale green in colour, but turning red as they ripen. They can be served raw in salads, grilled, or used as an ingredient in hot meat dishes.

Lor peyniri: goat's milk cheese. *See also page 71.*

Mint, dried *(nane)*: an essential seasoning in Turkish cuisine. *See also page 114.*

Nane: dried mint.

Nigella: *scc Çörckotu.*

Oklava: long, thin rolling pin between 1.5 and 2 m long, used for rolling out thin pastry for *börek*, pies and *baklava*. If necessary, you can use a smooth, clean wooden broomstick instead.

Otlu peynir: a crumbly cream cheese flavoured with wild herbs, wild garlic and salt. This speciality is found around Lake Van in eastern Anatolia.

Palamut: bonito, a type of fish.

Pastırma: air-dried meat, thickly coated with a paste made from a mixture of spices. It can be eaten in thin slices, fried with eggs, or as an ingredient in chick-pea or lentil hotpots. *Pastırma* is a speciality of the city of Kayseri in central Anatolia. *See also page 105.*

Pekmez: a syrup made from boiled-down grape or apple juice, delicious mixed with *tahini* and eaten as a dip with flat bread.

Pepper purée *(biber salçası)*: a thick purée of red peppers, usually hot and spicy, sold ready-made. *Sambal ulek*, the fiery Indonesian condiment, is a good substitute.

Phyllo: a type of wafer-thin pastry (also called filo) made from flour, salt and water. It is buttered and wrapped in multiple layers around both sweet and savoury fillings.

Pilav: a rice dish.

Pine nuts *(çamfıstığı)*: small nuts, also known as pine kernels or seeds. An essential part of Mediterranean cooking, they are used in rice-based stuffing and desserts.

Pirinç: uncooked rice.

Pulbiber (flaked peppers): coarsely ground, medium hot, red peppers, looking like little flakes. They are widely used to add flavour to various grilled meat and Turkish pizza. *See also page 115*

Rakı: strong spirit distilled from grapes and flavoured with aniseed.

Reçel: a kind of jam, produced by boiling fruit, vegetables, rose petals or bergamot rind in sugar syrup. *See also page 136.*

Ridge cucumber: green, tender and very crisp cucumber, usually used for making pickles in Britain. The larger cucumbers are not cultivated in Turkey.

Rose water *(gül suyu)*: the distilled essence of rose petals, used to flavour pastry. It is a speciality of the Isparta district of central Anatolia. Available from Middle Eastern or Greek specialist food shops, or from chemists. Some patisseries make their own.

Saç: a round, slightly domed, iron baking sheet, used with the domed side upwards to make a large flat bread known as *saç ekmeği,* and *yufka*—sheets of very thin, crisp pastry for pies. The *saç* can be turned over and the hollow side used as a pan to fry meat for dishes such as *saç kavurması* (shepherd's sandwiches).

Saç ekmeği: large, thin, flat bread, baked in Turkish villages on a *saç*, a domed baking sheet.

Salamura yaprak: vine leaves.

Salep: a traditional, rather thick, winter drink made from hot milk, sugar and *salep* (the ground root of the salep orchid, *orchis mascula*) and sprinkled with a little ground cinnamon. In winter salep is taken as a remedy for colds.

Sambal ulek: fiery Indonesian condiment.

Şarap: wine.

Sarımsaklı: seasoned with garlic.

Semizotu: purslane. This small plant, with reddish stems and thick, fleshy rounded leaves, has a sour nutty flavour and is eaten raw or sautéed. *See also page 42.*

Şerbet: refreshing, chilled, home-made soft drink made from the juice of fruit or berries, served on special occasions, for example to celebrate the birth of a baby.

Sesame: oil-rich seeds of a herbaceous plant, often roasted to bring out their nutty flavour. *See also page 49.*

Sucuk: dried garlic sausage with a firm texture, made from beef, lamb or a combination of the two. It can be fried or added to bean or lentil stews.

Sumak: reddish purple powder made from berries of the wild *rhus coriacaea* bush, used mainly as a salad seasoning.

Tahini: sesame paste made from husked, roasted and ground sesame seeds. Sold in jars, it is most commonly used in sauces and for making *hummus*. If *tahini* is left to stand, the solids separate from the oil, so it should be stirred thoroughly before use. *See also page 49.*

Tarhana: soup base, usually home-made, of burghul, yogurt and salt, sometimes enriched with tomatoes or onions or similar strongly flavoured ingredients. *See also page 34.*

Tel kadayif: thin strands of pastry that look like shredded wheat (also known as angel's pastry), used in sweet pastries such as *künefe*, angel's hair dessert. It is available from Middle Eastern or Greek specialist food shops. *See also page 128.*

Tulum peyniri: crumbly, white, salty, ewe's or goat's milk cheese, a typical product of the *yayla*, the alpine pastures where the herdsmen take their flocks in the spring. The cheese is hung in a *tulum*, a goatskin sack (plastic sacks are also used these days) so that it is pressed by its own weight. *See also page 71.*

Turşu: vegetables or fruit pickled in salt water, or a blend of salt water and vinegar. *Turşu* is available ready-made in jars from Middle Eastern specialist food shops. *See also page 55.*

Vine leaves, preserved: the leaves of the grape vine which grows in the Middle East are edible and are used to wrap and to decorate food. Vine leaves preserved in brine—*salamura yaprak*—are served stuffed in Turkey.

Yayla: grassy summer pastures in the mountains. The word has also come to mean a holiday village. *See also page 27.*

Yogurt: yogurt, a dairy product to which certain bacteria were added to sour the milk, was an invention of the Turkish tribes of central Asia. It is now widely used in Turkish cookery and in the cuisine of central Asia. Families in rural areas usually make their own. As a "starter", stir 1 to 2 heaped tablespoons of live yogurt into 1 litre milk, heated to about 25°C. Wrap the pot in cloth, cover it, and leave it to stand for about 12 hours in a warm place, until the milk thickens.

Yufka: round sheets of pastry, rolled out paper-thin and used for *börek*—filled pastries. *Sigara böreği* (cigarette böreks) *(recipe, page 66)* are fried *yufka* rolls.

Zeytin: olives.

Zeytinyağı: olive oil.

Zeytinyağlı: cooked with olive oil.

CONVERSION CHART

These figures are not exact equivalents, but have been rounded up or down slightly to make measuring easier.

Weight Equivalents

Metric	Imperial
15 g	½ oz
30 g	1 oz
60 g	2 oz
90 g	3 oz
125 g	¼ lb
150 g	5 oz
200 g	7 oz
250 g	½ lb
350 g	¾ lb
500 g	1 lb
1 kg	2 to 2¼ lb

Volume Equivalents

Metric	Imperial
8 cl	3 fl oz
12.5 cl	4 fl oz
15 cl	¼ pint
17.5 cl	6 fl oz
25 cl	8 fl oz
30 cl	½ pint
35 cl	12 fl oz
45 cl	¾ pint
50 cl	16 fl oz
60 cl	1 pint
1 litre	35 fl oz

Recipe Index

TIME-LIFE BOOKS

COOKERY AROUND THE WORLD
English edition staff for *Turkey*
Editorial: Luci Collings, Felicity Jackson and Kate Cann
Designer: Dawn McGinn
Production: Emma Wishart, Justina Cox
Technical Consultant: Michael A. Barnes

English translation by Isabel Varea for Ros Schwartz Translations, London

Published originally under the title *Küchen der Welt: Türkei* by Gräfe und Unzer Verlag GmbH, Munich © 1994 Gräfe und Unzer Verlag GmbH, Munich

This edition published by Time-Life Books B.V. Amsterdam
Authorized English language edition © 1995 Time-Life Books B.V.
First English language printing 1995

TIME-LIFE is a trademark of Time Warner Inc. U.S.A.

ISBN 0 7054 1207 5

GRÄFE UND UNZER

EDITORS: Dr. Stephanie von Werz-Kovacs and Birgit Rademacker
Editor-in-chief: Monika Arndt
Designer: Konstantin Kern
Recipes tested by: Monika Arndt
Setting and production: BuchHaus Robert Gigler GmbH
Cartography: Huber, Munich

Funda Engin, the author, grew up on the Bosphorus and has enjoyed cookery from an early age, having been largely taught by her cosmopolitan mother. She has travelled extensively throughout Turkey, collecting traditional recipes. Her choices for this book include regional specialities as well as a selection originating from the refined palace cuisine of Istanbul, shared here with readers for the first time. Funda Engin has also published a number of travel guides to Turkey.

Michael Brauner, who photographed the food for this volume, is a graduate of the Berlin Fotoschule. He worked as an assistant to several French and German photographers before setting up on his own in 1984. He now divides his time between his studios in Munich, Karlsruhe and Gordes in Provence.

Detlef Kellermann is a freelance artist and illustrator based in Aachen. A varied and versatile artist, his work has included designing stage sets and mosaics. The watercolours which he has created for this book reflect his love for Turkey, one of his favourite countries.

Picture Credits

Colour illustrations: Detlef Kellermann

All photographs were taken by Michael Brauner, Food Fotografie, unless indicated below:

Cover: Graham Kirk, London. 4 top (marketplace): Taneli Türkkan, Bernried; bottom (Turkish boys): real bild, Klaus-D. Neumann, Munich. 4-5 top (coffee house): Klaus-D. Neumann, Munich; centre (weaving a kilim): Silvestris Fotoservice, Kastl/Lughofer; bottom (Daçta harbour): Wilkin Spitta, Loham. 8-9 (veiled woman at the Eyüp-Sultan Mosque, Istanbul): José Poblete, Oberursel. 10: Gerhard P. Müller, Dortmund. 11 (2): Wilkin Spitta, Loham. 12 top: Taneli Türkkan, Bernried; bottom: Gerhard P. Müller, Dortmund. 13 top: José Poblete, Oberursel; bottom: Silvestris Fotoservice, Kastl/Lughofer. 14: Gerhard P. Müller, Dortmund. 15 top: Dr Janicke, jd, Munich; bottom: Taneli Türkkan, Bernried. 16: José Poblete, Oberursel. 17 top: real bild, Klaus-D. Neumann, Munich; bottom: Silvestris Fotoservice, Valentin. 18: Silvestris Fotoservice, Valentin. 19, 20: Gerhard P. Müller, Dortmund. 21 top: Taneli Türkkan, Bernried; bottom: José Poblete, Oberursel. 22: Wilkin Spitta, Loham. 23 top: Silvestris Fotoservice, Valentin; bottom: Heinz Wohner, Dortmund. 27: Dr Janicke, jd, Munich. 31: José Poblete, Oberursel. 55, 60: Taneli Türkkan, Bernried. 67: Gerhard P. Müller, Dortmund. 93: Silvestris Fotoservice, Valentin. 114: Silvestris Fotoservice, Wurch. 136: Taneli Türkkan, Bernried.

Colour reproduction by Fotolito Longo, Bolzano, Italy
Typeset by A. J. Latham Limited, Dunstable, Bedfordshire, England
Printed and bound by Mondadori, Verona, Italy